OPPOSING VIEWPOINTS® IN WORLD HISTORY

THE FRENCH REVOLUTION

Laura K. Egendorf, *Book Editor*

Daniel Leone, *President*
Bonnie Szumski, *Publisher*
Scott Barbour, *Managing Editor*
Helen Cothran, *Senior Editor*

OPPOSING
VIEWPOINTS®
SERIES

GREENHAVEN
PRESS®

THOMSON
GALE

San Diego • Detroit • New York • San Francisco • Cleveland
New Haven, Conn. • Waterville, Maine • London • Munich

Cover credit: © The Art Archive/Musée du Château de Versailles/Dagli Orti
North Wind Picture Archives, 57, 86

LIBRARY OF CONGRESS CATALOGING-IN-PUBLICATION DATA

The French Revolution / Laura K. Egendorf, book editor.
    p. cm. — (Opposing viewpoints in world history series)
    Includes bibliographical references and index.
    ISBN 0-7377-1815-3 (lib. : alk. paper) — ISBN 0-7377-1816-1 (pbk. : alk. paper)
    1. France—History—Revolution, 1789–1799—Sources. I. Egendorf, Laura K.,
1973– . II. Series.
DC141.F728 2004
944.04—dc21
                                              2003055271

Printed in the United States of America

✳ **Contents**

Chapter 2: The Controversial Events of the French Revolution

Chapter 4: Historians Evaluate the French Revolution

✳ Foreword

On December 2, 1859, several hundred soldiers gathered at the outskirts of Charles Town, Virginia, to carry out, and provide security for, the execution of a shabbily dressed old man with a beard that hung to his chest. The execution of John Brown quickly became and has remained one of those pivotal historical events that are immersed in controversy. Some of Brown's contemporaries claimed that he was a religious fanatic who deserved to be executed for murder. Others claimed Brown was a heroic and selfless martyr whose execution was a tragedy. Historians have continued to debate which picture of Brown is closest to the truth.

The wildly diverging opinions on Brown arise from fundamental disputes involving slavery and race. In 1859 the United States was becoming increasingly polarized over the issue of slavery. Brown believed in both the necessity of violence to end slavery and in the full political and social equality of the races. This made him part of the radical fringe even in the North. Brown's conviction and execution stemmed from his role in leading twenty-one white and black followers to attack and occupy a federal weapons arsenal in Harpers Ferry, Virginia. Brown had hoped to ignite a large slave uprising. However, the raid begun on October 16, 1859, failed to draw support from local slaves; after less than thirty-six hours, Brown's forces were overrun by federal and local troops. Brown was wounded and captured, and ten of his followers were killed.

Brown's raid—and its intent to arm slaves and foment insurrection—was shocking to the South and much of the North. An editorial in the *Patriot*, an Albany, Georgia, newspaper, stated that Brown was a "notorious old thief and murderer" who deserved to be hanged. Many southerners expressed fears that Brown's actions were part of a broader northern conspiracy against the South— fears that seemed to be confirmed by captured letters documenting Brown's ties with some prominent northern abolitionists, some of whom had provided him with financial support. Such alarms also found confirmation in the pronouncements of some speakers such as writer Henry David Thoreau, who asserted that

Brown had "a perfect right to interfere by force with the slave-holder, in order to rescue the slave." But not all in the North defended Brown's actions. Abraham Lincoln and William Seward, leading politicians of the nascent Republican Party, both denounced Brown's raid. Abolitionists, including William Lloyd Garrison, called Brown's adventure "misguided, wild, and apparently insane." They were afraid Brown had done serious damage to the abolitionist cause.

Today, though all agree that Brown's ideas on racial equality are no longer radical, historical opinion remains divided on just what Brown thought he could accomplish with his raid, or even whether he was fully sane. Historian Russell Banks argues that even today opinions of Brown tend to split along racial lines. African Americans tend to view him as a hero, Banks argues, while whites are more likely to judge him mad. "And it's for the same reason—because he was a white man who was willing to sacrifice his life to liberate Black Americans. The very thing that makes him seem mad to white Americans is what makes him seem heroic to Black Americans."

The controversy over John Brown's life and death remind readers that history is replete with debate and controversy. Not only have major historical developments frequently been marked by fierce debates as they happened, but historians examining the same events in retrospect have often come to opposite conclusions about their causes, effects, and significance. By featuring both contemporaneous and retrospective disputes over historical events in a pro/con format, the Opposing Viewpoints in World History series can help readers gain a deeper understanding of important historical issues, see how historical judgments unfold, and develop critical thinking skills. Each article is preceded by a concise summary of its main ideas and information about the author. An in-depth book introduction and prefaces to each chapter provide background and context. An annotated table of contents and index help readers quickly locate material of interest. Each book also features an extensive bibliography for further research, questions designed to spark discussion and promote close reading and critical thinking, and a chronology of events.

✳ **Introduction**

"[The French Revolutionaries] wanted freedom of thought, expression, religion, association, and of enterprise of all kinds. . . . They recognized their own program in the great Declaration of Rights of 1789. New rights, for more people, have been demanded ever since."

—Robert R. Palmer, history professor and author of *The World of the French Revolution*

Prior to 1789, the year the French Revolution began, the only nations with any true understanding of the modern conception of human rights were Great Britain and its former colony, the United States. To those two nations, the most important rights were political and civil rights—the right to participate in government, freedom of expression, and equality before the law. Human rights also encompass economic and social freedoms—the right to move out of the class into which one was born, for example, and to no longer be dependent on another's whims for one's livelihood (as was the case in the eighteenth century for French peasants whose income fluctuated not only due to each season's crops but also to the number of payments their feudal lords decided to charge). During the last decades of the eighteenth century, two segments of French society—women and the Third Estate (France's middle-class and poor)—sought to gain all of these rights—political, economic, and social—which had been largely withheld from them. Their efforts to transform France from a nation dominated by the king, clergy, and aristocrats into one that took into account the needs of the entire nation helped lead to the French Revolution. The revolution significantly altered French society, but only for a decade—unfortunately, by the turn of the nineteenth century, when Napoleon Bonaparte ascended to power, France had mostly reverted to its old ways. Several more revolutions were required until France successfully established a republic, a government for all the people.

Life Before the Revolution

In the years before the revolution, French women enjoyed virtually no civil or economic rights. As Darline Gay Levy, Harriet Branson Applewhite, and Mary Durham Johnson explain in the introduction to *Women in Revolutionary Paris, 1789–1795:* "By and large, women were legally totally subservient to their husbands or fathers in virtually all areas of marriage contracts, inheritance laws, property and tax laws, and child custody arrangements. Marriages were indissoluble." Noblewomen were not permitted to rule on disputes on properties they held. Meanwhile, working women lacked economic rights and protections; many were concerned about the entrance of men into traditionally female occupations such as seamstress and embroiderer. These women feared that unless such employment was restricted to females, the "fairer sex" would have to look for less respectable jobs.

Women were not the only people in France who were denied basic human rights, of course. Indeed, France's peasants lived under the worst conditions. Although industry was becoming a more important part of the nation's economy, France was still largely dependent on the feudal system in which powerful feudal lords (seigneurs) owned profitable farmlands on which peasants lived and worked. Some peasants had managed to earn enough money from their crops to purchase their own small plots of land, but the vast majority lived in poverty, completely under the thumbs of seigneurs. In his book *The Old Regime and the French Revolution*, nineteenth-century historian Alexis de Tocqueville details the burdens of the typical farmer:

> Everywhere the resident seigneur levied dues on fairs and markets, and everywhere enjoyed exclusive rights of hunting. . . . [It] was the general rule that farmers must bring their wheat to their lord's mill and the grapes to his wine press. A universal and very onerous right was that named *lods et*

ventes; that is to say an impost levied by the lord on transfers
of land within his domain. And throughout the whole of
France the land was subject to quitrents, ground rents, dues
in money or in kind payable by the peasant proprietor to his
lord and irredeemable by the former.

Not only did the peasants owe rent and crops to their feudal lords,
they also had to pay burdensome taxes to the government. By
comparison, as Gwynne Lewis explains in *The French Revolution:
Rethinking the Debate*, "The persistence of feudal social structures
meant that the real wealth of the country was not taxed: the great
landowners, the Church and the nobility, escaped most of the
taxes which fell upon land."

Even peasants who were landowners were far from comfortable
economically. As J.F. Bosher points out in his book, *The French
Revolution*, the typical rural family of five required sixty bushels
of wheat per year, "or with the triennial rotation of crops, about
15 acres of land for food." However, the majority of French peasants—as much as 70 percent in the region of Cambrésis, for example—owned less than two-and-a-half acres of farmland. To
make matters worse, France suffered several droughts and harsh
winters during the 1780s, and French peasants were unaware of
new, more efficient farming techniques; most used outdated tools
and methods that dated back to the Middle Ages.

While some peasants could at least hope that they would grow
enough grain to cover the money owed to their landlords and the
government and provide food for their family, the urban poor—
who, if not unemployed, worked primarily in factories and
shops—were dependent on the affordability and availability of
pre-baked bread. In the summer of 1787, a four-pound loaf, two
of which were required daily to feed a family of four, cost eight
sous. Due in large part to poor weather and low crop yields, by
February 1789 the price had nearly doubled to fifteen sous. In his
book *Citizens: A Chronicle of the French Revolution*, Simon
Schama notes: "The average [daily] wage of a manual laborer was
between twenty and thirty sous, of a journeyman mason at most
forty. The doubling of bread prices—and of firewood—spelled
destitution." Urban workers, especially those in Paris, started to

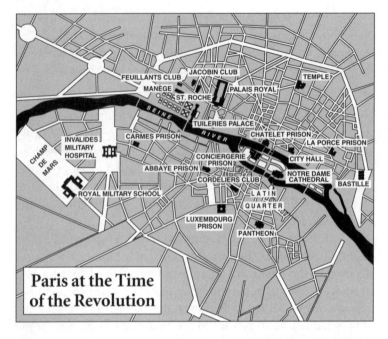

Paris at the Time of the Revolution

protest the price of bread. When two Parisian manufacturers, Réveillon and Henriot, suggested in late April 1789 that the distribution of bread should be deregulated, thereby lowering prices and reducing both wages and costs of production, riots ensued. Laborers—not only those who worked for bakers—took violent action against Réveillon and Henriot because they feared that other employers would use reduced bread prices as an excuse to cut their own workers' wages.

Another sector of French society that began to protest unequal treatment was the bourgeoisie, or middle class. Unlike the rural and urban poor, this economic class, whose members would prove so important during the revolution, had already begun to gain economic and social status before 1789. As France's population started its migration from country to town and factories began to dot the urban landscape, capitalists and financiers saw their wealth steadily increase. Middle-class children had more access to education and culture, and their upbringing brought them in closer contact to the French aristocracy, resulting in many marriages between the upper and middle classes. However, the growing economic strength of France's middle class was not accompanied by equal political power. Bourgeois members of the Third Estate were particularly aggrieved by the fact that the votes in the Estates-General (a legislative body convened on rare occasion by the king) were counted by estate, not head. Thus the Third Estate often found itself outvoted by the First Estate (clergy) and Second Estate (nobility), which usually voted together for measures that furthered their interests at the expense of the needs of the Third Estate. However, the Third Estate had twice as many deputies as either of the other two estates. Thus, had voting been done by a head count, all a unified Third Estate would need was a single vote from either the nobility or the clergy to establish a majority. An increased political voice was for most middle-class French people the most important human right to be attained. Albert Mathiez, a leading interpreter of the revolution, says of the middle class, "They were advancing steadily [economically]. . . . Their very rise made them more acutely sensitive to the inferior legal status to which they were still condemned."

Demanding Rights

The grievances of women, the rural and urban poor, and the middle class culminated in the French Revolution. The revolution began in 1789, with the first demands for greater rights made that January by French women. On January 1, 1789, King Louis XVI was presented with the Petition of Women of the Third Estate to the King. The rights demanded by the women included permission to send female deputies to the Estates-General, the right to an adequate education, and the right to earn a respectable living (and thus avoid drifting into prostitution). These demands were not especially radical—the petition made clear that they were not asking for equality with men. The petitioners explained, "We ask to be enlightened, to have work, not in order to usurp men's authority, but in order to be better esteemed by them." They added further, "We implore you, Sire, to set up free schools where we might learn our language on the basis of principles, religion and ethics. . . . Sciences? . . . they only serve to inspire us with a stupid pride, lead us to pedantry, go against the wishes of nature."

Other women, however, were more radical in their demands.

In September 1791 Marie Gouze, under the pseudonym Olympe de Gouges, published a pamphlet, the *Declaration of the Rights of Women*. The pamphlet, which was addressed to Queen Marie-Antoinette, asserted that women were entitled to seventeen rights, including property rights, free speech, and equal access to public and private "dignities, offices, and employments." Many women also expressed their political opinions in the salons, clubs that had flourished throughout the eighteenth century, where upper-class and middle-class women could gather with eminent writers and philosophers to discuss important issues.

For some women, however, gathering together to discuss politics with leading philosophers or writing revolutionary pamphlets was hardly practical. To the poorer women in Paris, access to affordable bread was the most important right. In October 1789 a large group of poor women marched to Versailles, the royal palace situated twelve miles beyond the capital, to demand bread, as supplies were limited within the city. Upon reaching the palace, a small delegation of women was granted an audience with King Louis XVI. The women eventually convinced the monarch to sign decrees agreeing to provide Paris with sufficient stores of affordable bread.

French women did not lack male support in their quest for human rights. One of the leading male voices for female political equality was Marie-Jean Caritat, the Marquis de Condorcet. Condorcet, a member of Paris's municipal assembly, expressed his support for women's rights in the July 1790 document, "On the Admission of Women to the Rights of Citizenship." Condorcet argued that, like men, women are able to acquire and analyze moral ideas and therefore are equally entitled to rights. He acknowledged that women may prefer to remain in the domestic sphere and perhaps are not as qualified for political office, but he maintained that such differences should not lead to unequal treatment. According to Condorcet:

> It is ... unjust to advance as grounds for continuing to refuse women the enjoyment of their natural rights those reasons that only have some kind of reality because women do not enjoy these rights in the first place. If one admits such argu-

> ments against women, it would also be necessary to take away
> the rights of citizenship from that portion of the people who,
> having to work without respite, can neither acquire enlight-
> enment nor exercise its reason, and soon little by little the
> only men who would be permitted to be citizens would be
> those who had followed a course in public law.

France's women met several of their early revolutionary goals. Levy, Applewhite, and Johnson conclude in their book that French women became politically influential; the three authors assert that the French government could no longer ignore their female subjects' demands. Women also benefited economically, with previously gender-biased laws on inheritance and property rights relaxed under the new regime. The divorce law of 1792 further improved women's civil status by setting seven grounds for divorce that women as well as men could use, including insanity, brutality, and abandonment. The new law made it equally easy for men and women to dissolve marriages quickly and inexpensively.

For peasants, change came swiftly and violently. In July 1789 France was wracked by what became known as the "Great Fear." On the fourteenth of that month, a riot at the Bastille, a Paris prison and armory, had resulted in the death of more than one hundred people. The riot began when the citizens of Paris—fearful that troops recently sent to the city by King Louis XVI might decide to attack the populace—began collecting weapons at the Bastille. Similar uprisings against the government followed. Rural citizens began hearing rumors that King Louis XVI was ordering his troops into the French countryside to stanch peasant rebellions. Fearful peasants began burning and pillaging manors, destroying feudal records, and reclaiming what had previously been common land. On August 4, 1789, worried that these demonstrations would not cease, the nation's nobles agreed to give up most of their feudal rights. This decision was codified one week later by the National Assembly. Peasants were now free to earn their own wages, unencumbered by feudal tithes; the economic element of human rights was becoming a reality for the nation's rural poor. The economic freedoms for urban laborers also widened during the revolution. The abolishment of guilds allowed artisans more opportunities to find jobs, unburdened by a complicated hierarchical system. Workshops established throughout cities were sources of employment for poor women. Urban laborers frequently went on strike, with higher wages a common result. Bread became more affordable; in 1793, the price of a loaf was six sous.

The first great triumph of the bourgeois was the reshaping of the Estates-General into the National Assembly. On May 5, 1789, King Louis XVI convened the Estates-General for its first meeting in 175 years to discuss solutions to France's economic woes. The delegates also debated on how voting should proceed and whether the system of representation should be altered. The Third Estate walked out of the meeting when the other two estates refused to change the traditional methods of voting. On June 17, 1789, the Third Estate held its own meeting and declared itself the National Assembly, inviting the delegates from the other two estates to join it. In the estimation of Nora Temple, author of *The Road to 1789: From Reform to Revolution in France*, the establishment of the National Assembly "[was] technically the beginning of the revolution because the Third Estate, and the few clergy who by that stage joined it, knew that they were claiming sovereign power when they assumed the title of National Assembly." A break from the monarchy, from what would be known as the Ancién Regime, had officially begun.

The second accomplishment of the National Assembly, and the one that had the greatest effect on the concept of modern human rights, was the adoption of the Declaration of the Rights of Man and Citizen on August 26, 1789. Debate about what to include in the document had begun earlier in the month, culminating in the decision to pare down the originally conceived twenty-four rights to seventeen. Assembly deputies argued over how much influence the United States's Declaration of Independence should have on the document; a chief disagreement was whether the American understanding of equality could be transferred successfully to a nation with a long history of aristocracy and feudalism. In the end, while the Declaration of the Rights of Man and Citizen was partly influenced by its American predecessor, the French document proved unique and enduring in its own way. Most important for many revolutionaries, was that the declaration helped the French middle class achieve its greatest goal: the codification of basic political, social, and civil rights.

Historians have long agreed that few documents have been more influential in Western history than the declaration. Geoffrey Best, the editor of *The Permanent Revolution: The French Revolution and Its Legacy, 1789–1989*, contends that the Declaration of the Rights of Man and Citizen was important because of its realistic understanding that in order to be beneficial, rights cannot be abstract. Rather, they must be codified in well-functioning constitutions. As Best opines, "Modern history is rich in instances of states with constitutions which read excellently, but in whose functioning there are hidden catches or practical failures which rubbish them as far as human rights go." Best further explains that the declaration was an important achievement because it was a document that expressed the rights of France as a people and as a nation, without regard to previous or current rulers. The opening paragraphs of the declaration help delineate what Lynn Hunt, in her introduction to *The French Revolution and Human Rights: A Brief Documentary History*, describes as the National Assembly's "vision of government based on principles completely different from those of the monarchy":

> [The] National Assembly recognizes and declares, in the presence and under the auspices of the Supreme Being, the following rights of man and citizen.
>
> 1. Men are born and remain free and equal in rights. Social distinctions can be based only upon public utility.
>
> 2. The aim of every political association is the preservation of the natural and imprescriptible [self-evident] rights of man. These rights are liberty, property, security, and resistance to oppression.
>
> 3. The source of all sovereignty is essentially in the nation; no body, no individual can exercise authority that does not proceed from it in plain terms.

The Declaration of the Rights of Man and Citizen has proved to be one of the most influential documents in history, one that has influenced the quest for human rights in not only Europe but throughout the world. Other accomplishments during the French Revolution turned out to be less enduring.

French women, who had benefited during the early stages of the revolution, found themselves at odds with the Jacobins, a radical party led by Maximilien de Robespierre and Georges Danton. The Jacobins rose to power in 1792 and established the first French Republic. Believing that women did not belong in the political sphere, the Jacobin government closed women's political clubs in November 1793. The Convention—the ruling body of the French Republic—had made its decision after hearing a report by André Amar, who suggested that it would be dangerous to give women too much political power. He declared, "Women are disposed by their organization to an over-excitation that would be deadly in public affairs. . . . Interests of state would soon be sacrificed to everything which ardor in passion can generate in the way of error and disorder."

Some of the more prominent revolutionary women lost not only their rights but also their lives. The Jacobin reign has been associated with the Reign of Terror, a nearly year-long stretch between the fall of 1793 and the summer of 1794 when the government arrested and executed more than twenty thousand people it believed were politically dangerous, including women whom it believed failed in their roles as obedient wives and mothers. Olympe de Gouges and Marie-Antoinette were among the victims. The lot of French women did not improve after the more moderate Thermidorians overthrew the Jacobin regime in July 1794. Women's workshops were disbanded in 1795, with the government urging women to work at home so they could become better wives and mothers.

The modest gains by the urban poor also proved short-lived. The decade-long revolution, which coincided with several wars against European foes, wracked France's already vulnerable economy. Affordable foodstuffs continued to be a problem for urban families. Despite the riots and the efforts of the Convention to guarantee adequate provisions for the urban poor, the high cost of bread remained a problem. In 1792 hoarding caused a rise in the cost of sugar. Levy, Applewhite, and Johnson explain, "Speculators hoarded vast stores of colonial products such as sugar, coffee, and tea in expectation of future profits from depleted supplies." Concerns over unequal allocations of eggs and butter led to riots in 1793. Urban workers lost the economic power they had gained when the National Assembly passed the Le Chapelier law in 1791, which prohibited all workers' coalitions and assemblies. A September 1793 law placed limits on wages. Freedom from hunger and want had been the right sought most fervently by the urban poor, but it was a right they were unable to enjoy.

The end of feudalism was on the surface a significant accomplishment for the peasants, who no longer suffered the burden of excessive dues and taxes. Yet not all peasants benefited equally from the revolution. Historian George Lefebvre points out that only well-off peasants could afford to purchase Church properties, which had become available for purchase when the National Assembly seized land held by clerics. Moreover, he explains, the lords who had dominated the countryside before the revolution were merely transformed by the revolution into landlords who still held most of the economic and political power in rural France. He writes, "The consequences of the Revolution from 1789 to the Terror were, for the most part, socially conservative. The effects of much of the legislation of this period played directly to the interests of groups who had done very well at the end of the old regime."

People of the French middle class had increased their economic power throughout the eighteenth century through trade and industry and had gradually gained social status via marriages into upper-class families. For this group, the primary revolutionary goal was to achieve a commensurate level of political strength. Once those desires were fulfilled with the passage of the Declaration of the Rights of Man and Citizen and the establishment of a government that did not favor the wealthy or the Church, the bourgeoisie had little else to demand. With the revolution being, at the end, essentially conservative, it is not surprising that the people from the middle classes who benefited the most were those who were able to enjoy the newfound wealth of land and business ownership that the revolution brought. As long as they remained economically strong, and as long as the monarchy and powerful aristocracy remained a thing of the past, the middle class seemed happy to remain where they were.

The revolution effectively came to an end on November 10, 1799, when Napoleon Bonaparte led a coup of the government and named himself the First Consul; he declared the revolution over on December 15. Emmanuel-Joseph Sieyès, who participated in that coup, penned a new constitution—one that made no mention of human rights or liberty, instead emphasizing peace, security, and property rights. The constitution was followed by the Napoleonic Code, a set of laws that purportedly guaranteed equality under the law but favored the wealthy. Napoleon's favoring of the wealthy continued throughout his reign. On March 1, 1808, Napoleon created more than three thousand noble titles. For a man who touted the idea of meritocracy—of people improving their social position through talent, not birth—Napoleon seemed to have a less-than-warm attitude toward the political and economic aspirations of France's lower classes. His consolidation of power ended the political freedoms of the bourgeois, as there was no longer a national legislature that the middle class could dominate.

The urban and rural poor were also affected under Napoleon's rule. Napoleon continued the ban on trade unions and introduced passbooks, which limited the ability of urban workers to move freely about the nation. However, he did set maximum prices for bread and flour, thus reducing the threat of either hunger or bread riots. According to Robert B. Holtman, author of *The Napoleonic Revolution*, peasants did not necessarily fare badly under Napoleon, as he maintained the work the revolutionaries had done (namely, abolishing feudalism). However, other scholars have asserted that Napoleon was largely uninterested in social and economic reforms that would improve the quality of life for his poorer subjects.

The Napoleonic Code also had a deleterious effect on women's rights. His rewriting of the divorce laws gave more control to husbands while advancements in inheritance and property rights were also swept away. Although French women later participated in their nation's nineteenth-century revolutions, they continued to lack basic political rights for many more decades; it was not until 1944 that they were given the right to vote.

New Revolutions

France's first attempt at a republic—at a government that would represent the interests of all its citizens, not just the privileged few—came to an end when Napoleon took over. His rule as France's dictator, and eventually its self-proclaimed emperor, ended in 1815 after his humiliating defeat at the Belgian town of Waterloo at the hands of England's Duke of Wellington, who led the combined forces of Britain, Belgium, Hanover, and the Netherlands against the French army. The French monarchy reemerged under the Restoration, when the Bourbon family returned to the throne, first with King Louis XVIII and then with Charles X, brothers of Louis XVI, and later in the nineteenth century with Louis Philippe. Napoleon's nephew Louis Napoleon Bonaparte followed his uncle's lead by declaring himself emperor in 1852.

Although the power of the first two kings was limited by constitutions (as had also been the case for Louis XVI during his final year as king), distaste for the return of the monarchy led to the revolutions of 1830 and 1848. During those revolutions, the French lower and middle classes fought to regain the rights they had acquired between 1789 and 1799. The Revolution of 1830 stemmed from fears that Charles X sought a return to an absolute monarchy. In July 1830 the king issued ordinances that limited the freedom of the press, dissolved the newly elected, liberal-dominated Chamber of Deputies (France's legislature), and reduced the number of eligible voters. Workers and the middle class demonstrated against the king, who soon fled to England. Louis Philippe, the Duke of Orleans, replaced him as king. Philippe's reign lasted until 1848. Frustration over a failing economy, political corruption, and voting restrictions led to the Revolution of 1848, France's third revolution in sixty years. Finally, after a revolution in 1870, France was able to establish a republic, and that system of government has remained intact for over 130 years, except for a period of four years when the Nazis occupied the country during World War II.

British poet William Wordsworth wrote in his 1804 poem, "French Revolution As It Appears to Enthusiasts," "Bliss was it in that dawn to be alive! But to be young was very heaven!" For France's women, poor, and middle class, the early years of the revolution may indeed have seemed heavenly. They found themselves free to declare their wishes for a political and economic voice in a new France. However, as the revolution continued, the actions of the fledging republic's leadership clearly showed that the new leaders' belief in human rights spread to the upper- and middle-class male but no further. The freedom experienced by France's less-privileged groups, though brief, ultimately whetted their appetite for more liberty. The French Revolution that began in 1789 may have ended in 1799, but the desire of its citizens for freedom would continue for decades beyond.

In *Opposing Viewpoints in World History: The French Revolution*, contributors evaluate the causes, controversies, and effects of the revolution in the following chapters: The Causes of the Revolution, The Controversial Events of the Revolution, Social Change in Revolutionary France, Historians Evaluate the French Revolution. In their viewpoints the authors show how the quest for human rights expanded beyond Great Britain and the United States to include a third nation, one determined to move from monarchy to modernity.

CHAPTER 1

The Causes of the French Revolution

✵ Chapter Preface

The causes of the French Revolution are complex; many of them can be traced far back into history. Indeed, the groundwork for the French Revolution was laid long before King Louis XVI, Maximilien Robespierre, and other key figures of the era reached adulthood. One such contributor to the revolution was the Enlightenment. This seventeenth- and eighteenth-century philosophical movement, whose adherents believed in freedom and equality, led to the popular belief in the 1780s that France should renounce monarchy and support a new type of government—one based on representation and consent. Although some historians have noted that Enlightenment philosophers were more conservative than the revolutionaries who were later inspired by their writings, the ideas of the Enlightenment took root in a nation eager to break away from traditional beliefs.

For hundreds of years the French had believed in the "divine right of kings"—the idea that a king's authority came directly from God and that the monarch was accountable to no one other than God. In 1690 British philosopher John Locke argued in direct opposition to this idea in his influential essay "Of Civil Government." Locke contended that political power is delivered through people, not a higher being. He argued that governments are legitimate only through the consent of the ruled and that the purpose of governments is to guarantee "the peace, safety, and public good of the people." In another essay, "Two Treatises of Government," Locke argued against the notion of absolute monarchy and in support of freedom and equality.

His writings proved influential in France, particularly among a group of thinkers known as *philosophes.* John H. Stewart, in his book *A Documentary Survey of the French Revolution*, suggests that France was most susceptible to Locke's views because "[its] middle class was most numerous, most prosperous, and most desirous of change." Political theorists such as Jean-Jacques Rousseau and Charles de Secondat (better known as the Baron de Montesquieu) ignored threats of censorship and began to write on politics and expand upon Locke's ideas. Rousseau's 1762 work *The Social Contract* was premised on the notion that republics were the best form of government. According to Rousseau, "The people, being subject to the laws, ought to be their author: the conditions of the society ought to be regulated solely by those who come together to form it." Montesquieu explored the need for checks and balances in his 1748's *Spirit of the Laws*. Stewart notes that Montesquieu believed France could support a monarchy if the executive, legislative, and judicial branches were separated. In *Spirit of the Laws*, Montesquieu asserts: "When the legislative and executive powers are united in the same person, or in the same body of magistrates, there can be no liberty; because apprehensions may arise, lest the same monarch or senate should enact tyrannical laws, to execute them in a tyrannical manner."

By 1780 France was beginning to feel the full effect of the *philosophes*. Their ideas were disseminated through pamphlets and in cafés and the intellectual gathering places known as *salons*. Daniel Mornet, the author of *French Thought in the Eighteenth Century*, explains: "Toward 1780 the philosophers might be feared and detested; but they could not be ignored. On their side they had the prestige of fashion and popularity." Yet ironically, as Mornet notes, the philosophers were not themselves revolutionary: "[Not] one of the philosophers could be considered a revolutionist. . . . Yet philosophy did play a very definite role. It taught neither revolution nor democracy. But it transformed men's minds; it made them lose the habit of respect for tradition."

Within nine years the transformation effected by the philosophers—regardless of their relative conservatism—had helped set the stage for the French Revolution. In the following chapter the authors debate the causes of one of the defining events in world history. As an examination of the influence of Enlightenment philosophers and their protegés makes clear, the French Revolution was not a sudden explosion in the summer of 1789; rather, it was the end result of nearly a century of changing ideas.

Viewpoint 1

"The fresh ruins of France . . . are the sad but instructive monuments of rash and ignorant counsel in time of profound peace."

Revolting Against the Monarchy Was an Irrational Act

Edmund Burke

One of the most notable evaluators of the French Revolution was the British statesman and orator Edmund Burke. In 1790 he published the book *Reflections on the Revolution in France*. In the following viewpoint, excerpted from that work, Burke criticizes the decision of the French citizenry to revolt against the monarchy of Louis XVI. According to Burke, starting the French Revolution was a rash and irrational act. He contends that France should have built upon its existing constitution and society instead of turning to violence against a lawful king. The immediate result of the revolution, according to Burke, was to impoverish the French people and plunge them into chaos.

[The English] political system is placed in a just correspondence and symmetry with the order of the world, and with

Edmund Burke, *Reflections on the Revolution in France*, 1790.

the mode of existence decreed to a permanent body composed of transitory parts; wherein, by the disposition of a stupendous wisdom, moulding together the great mysterious incorporation of the human race, the whole, at one time, is never old, or middle-aged, or young, but in a condition of unchangeable constancy, moves on through the varied tenour of perpetual decay, fall, renovation, and progression. Thus, by preserving the method of nature in the conduct of the state, in what we improve we are never wholly new; in what we retain we are never wholly obsolete. By adhering in this manner and on those principles to our forefathers, we are guided not by the superstition of antiquarians, but by the spirit of philosophic analogy. In this choice of inheritance we have given to our frame of polity the image of a relation in blood; binding up the constitution of our country with our dearest domestic ties; adopting our fundamental laws into the bosom of our family affections; keeping inseparable, and cherishing with the warmth of all their combined and mutually reflected charities, our state, our hearths, our sepulchres, and our altars.

Through the same plan of a conformity to nature in our artificial institutions, and by calling in the aid of her unerring and powerful instincts, to fortify the fallible and feeble contrivances of our reason, we have derived several other, and those no small benefits, from considering our liberties in the light of an inheritance. Always acting as if in the presence of canonized forefathers, the spirit of freedom, leading in itself to misrule and excess, is tempered with an awful gravity. This idea of a liberal descent inspires us with a sense of habitual native dignity, which prevents that upstart insolence almost inevitably adhering us and disgracing those who are the first acquirers of any distinction. By this means our liberty becomes a noble freedom. It carries an imposing and majestic aspect. It has a pedigree and illustrating ancestors. It has its bearings and its ensigns armorial. It has its gallery of portraits; its monumental inscriptions; its records, evidences, and titles. We procure reverence to our civil institutions on the principle upon which nature teaches us to revere individual men; on account of their age; and on account of those from whom they are descended. All your sophisters cannot produce any thing better adapted to preserve a rational and manly freedom than the course that we have pursued, who have chosen our nature rather than our speculations, our breasts rather than our inventions, for the great conservatories and magazines of our rights and privileges.

An Example for the French

You might, if you pleased, have profited of our example, and have given to your recovered freedom a correspondent dignity. Your privileges, though discontinued, were not lost to memory. Your constitution, it is true, whilst you were out of possession, suffered waste and dilapidation; but you possessed in some parts the walls, and in all the foundations of a noble and venerable castle. You might have repaired those walls; you might have built on those old foundations. Your constitution was suspended before it was perfected; but you had the elements of a constitution very nearly as good as could be wished. In your old states you possessed that variety of parts corresponding with the various descriptions of which your community was happily composed; you had all that combination, and all that opposition of interests, you had that action and counteraction which, in the natural and in the political world, from the reciprocal struggle of discordant powers, draws out the harmony of the universe. These opposed and conflicting interests, which you considered as so great a blemish in your old and in our present constitution, interpose a salutary check to all precipitate resolutions; They render deliberation a matter not of choice, but of necessity; they make all change a subject of *compromise*, which naturally begets moderation; they produce *temperaments*, preventing the sore evil of harsh, crude, unqualified reformations; and rendering all the headlong exertions of arbitrary power, in the few or in the many, for ever impracticable. Through that diversity of members and interests, general liberty had as many securities as there were separate views in the several orders; whilst by pressing down the whole by the weight of a real monarchy, the separate parts would have been prevented from warping and starting from their allotted places.

You had all these advantages in your antient states; but you chose to act as if you had never been moulded into civil society, and had every thing to begun anew. You began ill, because you began by despising every thing that belonged to you. You set up your trade without a capital. If the last generations of your country appeared without much lustre in your eyes, you might have passed them by, and derived your claims from a more early race of ancestors. Under a pious predilection for those ancestors, your imaginations would have realized in them a standard of virtue and wisdom, beyond the vulgar practice of the hour: and you would have risen with the example to whose imitation you aspired. Respecting your forefathers, you would have been taught to respect yourselves. You would not have chosen to consider the French as a people of yesterday, as a nation of low-born servile wretches until the emancipating year of 1789. In order to furnish, at the expence of your honour, an excuse to your apologists here for several enormities of yours, you would not have been content to be represented as a gang of Maroon [fugitive] slaves, suddenly broke loose from the house of bondage, and therefore to be pardoned for your abuse of the liberty to which you were not accustomed and ill fitted. Would it not, my worthy friend, have been wiser to have you thought, what I, for one, always thought you, a generous and gallant nation, long misled to your disadvantage by your high and romantic sentiments of fidelity, honour, and loyalty; that events had been unfavourable to you, but that you were not enslaved through any illiberal or servile disposition; that in your most devoted submission, you were actuated by a principle of public spirit, and that it was your country you worshipped, in the person of your king? Had you made it to be understood, that in the delusion of this amiable error you had gone further than your wise ancestors; that you were resolved to resume your ancient privileges, whilst you preserved the spirit of your ancient and your recent loyalty and honour; or, if diffident of yourselves, and not clearly discerning the almost obliterated constitution of your ancestors, you had looked to your neighbours in this land, who had kept alive the ancient principles and models of the old common law of Europe meliorated and adapted to its present state—by following wise examples you would have given new examples of wisdom to the world. You would have rendered the cause of liberty venerable in the eyes of every worthy mind in every nation. You would have shamed despotism from the earth, by shewing that freedom was not only reconcileable, but as, when well disciplined it is, auxiliary to law. You would have had an unoppressive but a productive revenue.

You would have had a flourishing commerce to feed it. You would have had a free constitution; a potent monarchy; a disciplined army; a reformed and venerated clergy; a mitigated but spirited nobility, to lead your virtue, not to overlay it; you would have had a liberal order of commons, to emulate and to recruit that nobility; you would have had a protected, satisfied, laborious, and obedient people, taught to seek and to recognize the happiness that is to be found by virtue in all conditions; in which consists the true moral equality of mankind, and not in that monstrous fiction, which, by inspiring false ideas and vain expectations into men destined to travel in the obscure walk of laborious life, serves only to aggravate and imbitter that real inequality, which it never can remove; and which the order of civil life establishes as much for the benefit of those whom it must leave in an humble state, as those whom it is able to exalt to a condition more splendid, but not more happy. You had a smooth and easy career of felicity and glory laid open to you, beyond any thing recorded in the history of the world; but you have shewn that difficulty is good for man.

A Disgraceful Situation

Compute your gains: see what is got by those extravagant and presumptuous speculations which have taught your leaders to despise all their predecessors, and all their contemporaries, and even to despise themselves, until the moment in which they became truly despicable. By following those false lights, France has bought undignified calamities at a higher price than any nation has purchased the most unequivocal blessings! France has bought poverty by crime! France has not sacrificed her virtue to her interest; but she has abandoned her interest, that she might prostitute her virtue. All other nations have begun the fabric of a new government, or the reformation of an old, by establishing originally, or by enforcing with greater exactness some rites or other of religion. All other people have laid the foundations of civil freedom in severer manners, and a system of a more austere and masculine morality. France, when she let loose the reins of regal authority, doubled the licence, of a ferocious dissoluteness in manners, and of an insolent irreligion in opinions and practices; and has extended through all ranks of life, as if she were communicating some privilege, or laying open some secluded benefit, all the unhappy corruptions that usually were the disease of wealth and power. This is one of the new principles of equality in France.

France, by the perfidy of her leaders, has utterly disgraced the tone of lenient council in the cabinets of princes, and disarmed it of its most potent topics. She has sanctified the dark suspicious maxims of tyrannous distrust; and taught kings to tremble at (what will hereafter be called) the delusive plausibilities, of moral politicians. Sovereigns will consider those who advise them to place an unlimited confidence in their people, as subverters of their thrones; as traitors who aim at their destruction, by leading their easy good-nature, under specious pretences, to admit combinations of bold and faithless men into a participation of their power. This alone (if there were nothing else) is an irreparable calamity to you and to mankind. Remember that your parliament of Paris told your king, that in calling the states together, he had nothing to fear but the prodigal excess of their zeal in providing for the support of the throne. It is right that these men should hide their heads. It is right that they should bear their part in the ruin which their counsel has brought on their sovereign and their country. Such sanguine declarations tend to lull authority asleep; to encourage it rashly to engage in perilous adventures of untried policy; to neglect those provisions, preparations, and precautions, which distinguish benevolence from imbecillity; and without which no man can answer for the salutary effect of any abstract plan of government or of freedom. For want of these, they have seen the medicine of the state corrupted into its poison. They have seen the French rebel against a mild and lawful monarch, with more fury, outrage, and insult, than ever any people has been known to rise against the most illegal usurper, or the most sanguinary tyrant. Their resistance was made to concession; their revolt was from protection; their blow was aimed at a hand holding out graces, favours, and immunities.

This was unnatural. The rest is in order. They have found their punishment in their success. Laws overturned; tribunals subverted; industry without vigour; commerce expiring; the revenue unpaid, yet the people impoverished; a church pillaged, and a state not relieved; civil and military anarchy made the constitution of the kingdom; every thing human and divine sacrificed to the idol of public credit, and national bankruptcy the consequence; and to crown all, the paper securities of new, precarious, tottering power, the discredited paper securities of impoverished fraud, and beggared rapine, held out as a currency for the support of an empire, in lieu of the two great recognized species that represent the lasting conventional credit of mankind, which disappeared and hid themselves in the earth from whence they came, when the principle of property, whose creatures and representatives they are, was systematically subverted.

A Rash and Ignorant Decision

Were all these dreadful things necessary? were they the inevitable results of the desperate struggle of determined patriots, compelled to wade through blood and tumult, to the quiet shore of a tranquil and prosperous liberty? No! nothing like it. The fresh ruins of France, which shock our feelings wherever we can turn our eyes, are not the devastation of civil war; they are the sad but instructive monuments of rash and ignorant counsel in time of profound peace. They are the display of inconsiderate and presumptuous, because unresisted and irresistible authority. The persons who have thus squandered away the precious treasure of their crimes, the persons who have made this prodigal and wild waste of public evils (the last stake reserved for the ultimate ransom of the state) have met in their progress with little, or rather with no opposition at all. Their whole march was more like a triumphal procession than the progress of a war. Their pioneers have gone before them, and demolished and laid every thing level at their feet. Not one drop of *their* blood have they shed in the cause of the country they have ruined. They have made no sacrifices to their projects of greater consequence than their shoe-buckles, whilst they were imprisoning their king, murdering their fellow citizens, and bathing in tears, and plunging in poverty and distress, thousands of worthy men and worthy families. Their cruelty has not even been the base result of fear. It has been the effect of their sense of perfect safety, in authorizing treasons, robberies, rapes, assassinations, slaughters, and burnings throughout their harrassed land. But the cause of all was plain from the beginning.

Viewpoint 2

"In the instance of France we see a revolution generated in the rational contemplation of the rights of man."

Revolting Against the Monarchy Was a Rational Act

Thomas Paine

Thomas Paine was an Anglo-American political philosopher known for pamphlets he wrote in support of the American Revolution. In 1791 he wrote *The Rights of Man*, a response to Edmund Burke's *Reflections on the Revolution in France*. In the following viewpoint, excerpted from his book, Paine defends the decision of French citizens to revolt against the monarchy. He argues that the French people were not rebelling against the person of King Louis XVI, who was a good king, but against the endemic despotism that marked all political, economic, and religious affairs in France. He contends that the French masses quite reasonably wanted to overcome this political and economic repression and establish new civil and political rights.

Thomas Paine, *The Rights of Man*, 1791.

Wꜱe now come more particularly to the affairs of France. Mr. [Edmund] Burke's book [*Reflections on the Revolution in France*] has the appearance of being written as instruction to the French Nation; but if I may permit myself the use of an extravagant metaphor, suited to the extravagance of the case, It is darkness attempting to illuminate light.

While I am writing this there are accidentally before me some proposals for a declaration of rights by the Marquis de la Fayette (I ask his pardon for using his former address, and do it only for distinction's sake) to the National Assembly, on the 11th of July, 1789, three days before the taking of the Bastille;[1] and I cannot but remark with astonishment how opposite the sources are from which that gentleman and Mr. Burke draw their principles. Instead of referring to musty records and mouldy parchments to prove that the rights of the living are lost, "renounced and abdicated for ever," by those who are now no more, as Mr. Burke has done, M. de la Fayette applies to the living world, and emphatically says, "Call to mind the sentiments which Nature has engraved in the heart of every citizen, and which take a new force when they are solemnly recognised by all: For a Nation to love Liberty, it is sufficient that she knows it; and to be free, it is sufficient that she wills it." How dry, barren, and obscure is the source from which Mr. Burke labours; and how ineffectual, though gay with flowers, are all his declamation and his arguments compared with these clear, concise, and soul-animating sentiments! Few and short as they are, they lead to a vast field of generous and manly thinking, and do not finish, like Mr. Burke's periods, with music in the ear, and nothing in the heart.

As I have introduced M. de la Fayette, I will take the liberty of adding an anecdote respecting his farewell address to the Congress of America in 1783, which occurred fresh to my mind, when I saw Mr. Burke's thundering attack on the French Revolution. M. de la Fayette went to America at an early period of the [American Revolutionary] war, and continued a volunteer in her ser-

---

1. The Bastille was a large fortress and prison located on the outskirts of Paris. On July 14, 1789, a large crowd of French citizens stormed the Bastille in search of weapons in case the king ordered his troops to attack the city.

vice to the end. His conduct through the whole of that enterprise is one of the most extraordinary that is to be found in the history of a young man, scarcely then twenty years of age. Situated in a country that was like the lap of sensual pleasure, and with the means of enjoying it, how few are there to be found who would exchange such a scene for the woods and wildernesses of America, and pass the flowery years of youth in unprofitable danger and hardship! But such is the fact. When the war ended, and he was on the point of taking his final departure, he presented himself to Congress, and contemplating, in his affectionate farewell, the Revolution he had seen, expressed himself in these words: "May this great monument raised to Liberty, serve as a lesson to the oppressor, and an example to the oppressed!" When this address came to the hands of Dr. [Benjamin] Franklin, who was then in France, he applied to Count Vergennes to have it inserted in the *French Gazette*, but never could obtain his consent. The fact was that Count Vergennes was an aristocratical despot at home, and dreaded the example of the American Revolution in France, as certain other persons now dread the example of the French Revolution in England; and Mr. Burke's tribute of fear (for in this light his book must be considered) runs parallel with Count Vergennes' refusal. But to return more particularly to his work—

"We have seen," says Mr. Burke, "the French rebel against a mild and lawful Monarch, with more fury, outrage, and insult, than any people has been known to rise against the most illegal usurper, or the most sanguinary tyrant." This is one among a thousand other instances, in which Mr. Burke shows that he is ignorant of the springs and principles of the French Revolution.

It was not against Louis XVI., but against the despotic principles of the government, that the Nation revolted. These principles had not their origin in him, but in the original establishment, many centuries back; and they were become too deeply rooted to be removed, and the Augean stable of parasites and plunderers too abominably filthy to be cleansed,[2] by anything short of a complete and universal Revolution. When it becomes necessary to do a

2. Paine is referring to the mythical figure Hercules, who was assigned twelve impossible tasks, including cleaning the Augean stables.

thing, the whole heart and soul should go into the measure, or not attempt it. That crisis was then arrived, and there remained no choice but to act with determined vigour, or not to act at all. The King was known to be the friend of the Nation, and this circumstance was favourable to the enterprise. Perhaps no man bred up in the style of an absolute King, ever possessed a heart so little disposed to the exercise of that species of power as the present King of France. But the principles of the Government itself still remained the same. The Monarch and the Monarchy were distinct and separate things; and it was against the established despotism of the latter, and not against the person or principles of the former, that the revolt commenced, and the Revolution has been carried.

Mr. Burke does not attend to the distinction between *men* and *principles;* and, therefore, he does not see that a revolt may take place against the despotism of the latter, while there lies no charge of despotism against the former.

The natural moderation of Louis XVI. contributed nothing to alter the hereditary despotism of the Monarchy. All the tyrannies of former reigns, acted under that hereditary despotism, were still liable to be revived in the hands of a successor. It was not the respite of a reign that would satisfy France, enlightened as she then was become. A casual discontinuance of the *practice* of despotism, is not a discontinuance of its *principles;* the former depends on the virtue of the individual who is in immediate possession of the power; the latter, on the virtue and fortitude of the nation. In the case of Charles I. and James II. of England, the revolt was against the personal despotism of the men; whereas in France, it was against the hereditary despotism of the established government. But men who can consign over the rights of posterity for ever on the authority of a mouldy parchment, like Mr. Burke, are not qualified to judge of this Revolution. It takes in a field too vast for their views to explore, and proceeds with a mightiness of reason they cannot keep pace with.

But there are many points of view in which this Revolution may be considered. When despotism has established itself for ages in a country, as in France, it is not in the person of the King only that it resides. It has the appearance of being so in show, and in nominal authority; but it is not so in practice and in fact. It has its standard everywhere. Every office and department has its despotism, founded upon custom and usage. Every place has its Bastille, and every Bastille its despot. The original hereditary despotism resident in the person of the King, divides and subdivides itself into a thousand shapes and forms, till at last the whole of it is acted by deputation. This was the case in France; and against this species of despotism, proceeding on through an endless labyrinth of office till the source of it is scarcely perceptible, there is no mode of redress. It strengthens itself by assuming the appearance of duty, and tyrannises under the pretence of obeying.

When a man reflects on the condition which France was in from the nature of her Government, he will see other causes for revolt than those which immediately connect themselves with the person or character of Louis XVI. There were, if I may so express it, a thousand despotisms to be reformed in France, which had grown up under the hereditary despotism of the monarchy, and became so rooted as to be in great measure independent of it. Between the Monarchy, the Parliament, and the Church, there was a *rivalship* of despotism; besides the feudal despotism operating locally, and the ministerial despotism operating everywhere. But Mr. Burke, by considering the King as the only possible object of a revolt, speaks as if France was a village, in which everything that passed must be known to its commanding officer, and no oppression could be acted but what he could immediately controul. Mr. Burke might have been in the Bastille his whole life, as well under Louis XVI. as Louis XIV., and neither the one nor the other have known that such a man as Mr. Burke existed. The despotic principles of the Government were the same in both reigns, though the dispositions of the men were as remote as tyranny and benevolence.

What Mr. Burke considers as a reproach to the French Revolution (that of bringing it forward under a reign more mild than the preceding ones) is one of its highest honours. The Revolutions that have taken place in other European countries, have been excited by personal hatred. The rage was against the man, and he became the victim. But, in the instance of France we see a revolution generated in the rational contemplation of the rights of man, and distinguishing from the beginning between persons and principles.

Viewpoint 3

"The public happiness is a source from which each has a right to draw his supply."

The Aristocrats Sought Greater Civil Rights for All French Citizens

Nobility of Blois

In the years before the revolution, the French aristocracy enjoyed many economic and political privileges, including the right to collect tithes from peasants who worked their lands. Despite their privileged position, many of the more liberal nobles were dismayed by the lack of political and civil rights afforded to the average French citizen and sought to redress the inequality. In the following viewpoint, excerpted from a letter addressed to the viscount of Beauharnois and the cavalier de Phelines, a group of nobles from the *bailliage* (royal court) of Blois argues that reforms are needed to ensure that all French people have the opportunity to pursue happiness. According to the aristocrats, these reforms include ending unlawful exiles and arrests, establishing a free press, creating a commission that will examine inequality in the judicial system, and ensuring that there is only one code of law throughout all of France.

Nobility of Blois, "Cahier of 1789," *Translations and Reprints from the Original Sources of European History*, edited by Merrick Whitcombe. Philadelphia: University of Pennsylvania, 1898.

The object of every social institution is to confer the greatest possible happiness upon those who live under its laws.

Happiness ought not to be confined to a small number of men; it belongs to all. It is not an exclusive privilege to be contested for; it is a common right which must be preserved, which must be shared, and the public happiness is a source from which each has a right to draw his supply.

Such are the sentiments which animate the nobility of the bailliage of Blois, at a moment when we are called upon by the sovereign to give our representatives to the nation. These principles have occupied all our thoughts during the preparation of this cahier. May they animate all citizens of this great state! May they evoke that spirit of union, that unanimity of desires which shall erect upon an indestrucible foundation of power the prosperity of the nation, the welfare of the monarch and his subjects!

Deep and established ills cannot be cured with a single effort: the destruction of abuses is not the work of a day. Alas! Of what avail to reform them if their causes be not removed? The misfortune of France arises from the fact that it has never had a fixed constitution. A virtuous and sympathetic king seeks the counsels and cooperation of the nation to establish one; let us hasten to accomplish his desires; let us hasten to restore to his soul that peace which his virtues merit. The principles of this constitution should be simple; they may be reduced to two: Security for person, security for property; because, in fact, it is from these two fertile principles that all organization of the body politic takes its rise.

Personal Liberty

Art. I. In order to assure the exercise of this first and most sacred of the rights of man, we ask that no citizen may be exiled, arrested or held prisoner except in cases contemplated by the law and in accordance with a decree originating in the regular courts of justice.

That in case the States General determine that provisional detention may be necessary at times, it ought to be ordained that every person so arrested shall be delivered, within twenty-four hours into the band of appropriate judges, to be judged with the least possible delay, in conformity with the laws of the kingdom; that evocations be abolished, and that no extraordinary commission be established in any instance; finally that no person be deprived of his position, civil or military, without judgment in due form.

Since individual liberty is a right equally sacred for citizens of all ranks and classes, without distinction or precedence, the States General are invited to interest themselves in the suppression of all forced service in the militia and of acts of authority which involve the violation of personal rights, and which are the more intolerable in a century of intelligence, when it is possible to accomplish the same end with less oppressive means. The application of these principles ought to suffer exception only in the case of an urgent necessity, when the safety of the country is at stake, in which case the extent of the executive power should be enlarged.

From the right of personal liberty arises the right to write, to think, to print and to publish, with the names of authors and publishers, all kinds of complaints and reflections upon public and private affairs, limited by the right of every citizen to seek in the established courts legal redress against author or publisher, in case of defamation or injury; limited also by all restrictions which the States General may see fit to impose in that which concerns morals and religion.

The violation of the secrecy of letters is still an infringement upon the liberty of citizens; and since the sovereign has assumed the exclusive right of transporting letters throughout the kingdom, and this has become a source of public revenue, such carriage ought to be made under the seal of confidence.

We indicate further a number of instances in which natural liberty is abridged:

1. The abuse of police regulations, which every year, in an arbitrary manner and without regular process, thrusts a number of artisans and useful citizens into prisons, work-houses and places of detention, often for trivial faults and even upon simple suspicion;

2. The abuse of exclusive privileges which fetter industry;

3. The guilds and corporations which deprive citizens of the right of using their faculties;

4. The regulations governing manufactures, the rights of inspection and marque, which impose restrictions that have lost their usefulness, and which burden industry with a tax that yields no profit to the public treasury. . . .

The Administration of Justice

Art. 3. The order of the nobility of the bailliage of Blois will review this subject briefly. We shall limit ourselves to observing that the administration of justice is less a privilege than a duty of sovereignty; that it ought to be gratuitous, at least to the poor, or in any event not expensive; that procedure should be simple and expeditious; that all useless stages of jurisdiction should be abolished; that in arranging the jurisdiction and fixing the competance of courts the convenience of litigants alone should be regarded, and not that of magistrates, since magistrates were constituted for the people, and not the people for the magistrates. That certain estimates, which have come to the notice of the nobility of the bailliage of Blois, respecting the enormous cost to the nation of the administration of justice, have produced upon us an impression of grief and horror.

That, through a neglect of constitutional principles, all powers of the state have been confounded with the judicial power; that under the pretext of judicial rulings the superior courts have assumed a portion of the legislative power; that under the pretext of police regulations the inferior courts, often times a single person bent upon following out his individual system, have been permitted to establish regulations which encroach upon the liberty of citizens and seriously affect the rights of property.

The attention of the order of nobility has been still more painfully directed to our criminal laws. Originating in a period of ignorance and barbarity, they reflect the ferocity of manners then prevailing. From the moment of his apprehension the accused is looked upon as guilty; counsel and assistance of all kinds are refused him.

A judge of original jurisdiction examines witnesses and receives depositions; and this testimony, received by a judge oftentimes ill instructed, sometimes prejudiced, becomes practically a sentence of death, from which the accused cannot hope to escape; for what assistance can the appellate court provide, when it determines only upon procedure, upon depositions received from the first judge?

It is not the duty of the nobility of the bailliage of Blois to attempt to present to the States General a plan for the reformation of the civil and criminal laws. There will not be wanting virtuous, sensible and enlightened magistrates, gathered from all provinces of the kingdom, who will make their voices heard in that august assembly.

We limit ourselves to demand that there shall be appointed, at the opening of the coming assembly of the States General, a commission composed of persons of enlightenment, whose business it shall be to take this matter into consideration. This commission ought not to be composed exclusively of magistrates and jurists; the most distinguished virtue is not beyond the seduction of prejudice. There ought to be included citizens of all estates and orders, particularly of those who have had the privilege of studying the English system of criminal jurisprudence.

We shall not close this article without asking:

1. That legal forms accompanying actions arising from the seizure and sale of property, administrations and creditors' mandates, and other actions in which a large number of persons are interested, shall be abridged and simplified;

2. That the file of notarial records shall be sacred; that they shall be placed, after an interval of time has elapsed, in a public place, where all citiens may have access to them;

3. That there shall be established in each rural parish, a court of reconciliation, composed of the seigneur, the parish priest and certain elderly men, for the purpose of amicably settling disputes and preventing suits at law. . . .

Special Matters

Art 7. The nobility of the bailliage of Blois, in commencing the composition of these instructions, had nothing further in view than the tracing of a plan of constitution most conformable to the principles of monarchy, and most likely to ensure to the nation the free exercise of its legitimate rights; we proposed, moreover, to confine ourselves to general considerations. The great number of suggestions and memorials, however, which have been sent in by various members of the order during the progress of our labors, has gradually diverted us from our earlier plan, and it seems to us desirable to include a number of felicitous ideas and important reflections, which do honor to the knowledge and patriotic spirit of their originators. Fearing, however, that they might lose somewhat of their original force or be inadequately developed in our presentation, we have determined that the original memorials themselves should be turned over to the deputies. The leading ideas which we have extracted from these writings, and which we have determined to incorporate in our demands, are the following:

1. The augmentation, out of the funds of the clergy, of the salary of parish priests with minimum dotation, the greater part of whom are in a state bordering so close upon poverty that they often share in the misery of the country people, without being able to relieve it.

2. That the law exempting from the payment of taille each rural inhabitant who has twelve children be re-enacted, and in case of the total suppression of the taille some equivalent compensation be made.

3. Throughout the whole kingdom there should be but one code of laws, one system of weights and measures.

4. That a commission be established composed of the most eminent, men of letters of the capital and provinces, and citizens of all orders, to formulate a plan of national education for the benefit of all classes of society; and for the purpose of revising elementary text-book.

5. That all customs duties collected in the interior of the kingdom be abolished, and all custom-houses, offices and customs barriers be removed to the frontier.

6. That rank, power or credit shall not be permitted to avert the rigors of the law in the case of fraudulent bankruptcies, and that the custom of issuing writs of suspension be done away with, at least until they have been demanded by the creditors themselves.

7. That any bill signed by a nobleman be declared a bill of honor.

8. That the troops be employed upon the highways and public works.

9. That there be established in country parishes, at the expense of seigneurs who demand it, retreats for disabled soldiers, for which the king shall furnish only the clothing.

10. That the law prohibiting all persons not noble from carrying arms be put in force, and that precautions be taken to assure its execution.

11. That the mounted police be increased, and that projects

which have been advanced looking to an establishment of foot brigades be considered.

With regard to all that concerns public charities, mendicancy, hospitals, foundling asylums and other benevolent institutions, the assembly of the nobility recognizes their importance, but considers itself not in duty bound to take them into consideration, since they are more especially within the jurisdiction of the provincial estates.

Further Abuses Must Be Prevented

Art. 8. Up to this point we have merely indicated the abuses which have accumulated in France during a long succession of centuries; we have made it evident that the rights of citizens have been abridged by a multitude of laws which attack property, liberty and personal safety.

That these rights have suffered injury as well in the nature as in the imposition of the taxes; in the administration of justice in both civil and criminal law; that this has been the case especially in the administration of the public revenues.

It is not sufficient to suppress these abuses; it is necessary to prevent their return; there must be established in ever-active influence, moving without interruption in the direction of public prosperity, which shall bear in itself the germ of all good, a principle destructive of all evil.

Viewpoint 4

"Is it not clear that if [the Third Estate's] influence is less than equal it cannot hope to escape from its political nonexistence and become something?"

The Middle Class Sought Increased Political Rights

Emmanuel Joseph Sieyès

Prior to the French Revolution, the nation's inhabitants were divided into three "estates," or orders. The First Estate, or the clergy, was comprised of 130,000 people; the Second Estate was the aristocracy, which numbered 110,000. The remaining 25 million belonged to the Third Estate, which consisted of the middle class and poor, who lacked the political and economic freedoms of the first two groups. In 1788 and 1789 the Third Estate, especially the segment known as the *bourgeoisie*, or middle class, began to seek a greater political voice.

In January 1789 Emmanuel Joseph Sieyès, a priest, political theorist, and major figure in the revolution, published the pamphlet *What Is the Third Estate?* In the following viewpoint, which features excerpts from that pamphlet, Sieyès explains the political demands of the French middle class. According to Sieyès the Third Estate wants equal representation in the Estates-General, a

Emmanuel Joseph Sieyès, "What Is the Third Estate?" January 1789.

legislative assembly occasionally convened by the king. The commoners want the votes in the Estates-General to be taken by head, not by group, because the aristocracy and clergy tend to vote in tandem against the commoners. Sieyès further argues that in order to achieve political equality, the number of Third Estate representatives must be at least equal to the sum of those in the first two estates and that these legislators must be educated, honest, and not beholden to the clergy or nobility.

One must not judge [the Third Estate's] demands from isolated observations of a few authors more or less educated about the rights of man. The Third Estate is still very backward in this respect, by which I mean not only in comparison with those who have studied the social order, but even in comparison with the mass of commonly held ideas that form public opinion. One can only come to appreciate the real complaints of this order by studying the formal demands addressed to the government by the large municipalities of the kingdom. What does one see there? That the people want to be *something*, and actually, they ask very little. They want to have real representatives in the Estates General,[1] meaning deputies *drawn from their order*, who are capable of being interpreters of their wishes and defenders of their interests. But what would be the use of their being present in the Estates General if interests contrary to theirs were to predominate! Their presence would only sanction the oppression of which they would be the eternal victims. Therefore, it is indeed certain that they cannot come to the Estates General to vote unless they can have *influence at least equal to that of the privileged*, and they demand a number of representatives equal to those of the other two orders [the clergy and aristocracy] together. Finally, this equality of representation would become perfectly illusory if each chamber had its separate vote. The Third therefore demands that the votes be taken *by head and not by order*. There you have the essence of the claims that have seemed to alarm the privileged, because the lat-

1. A legislative assembly that existed prior to the revolution.

ter have thought their mere acceptance sufficient to make reform of abuses unavoidable. The real intention of the Third Estate is to have in the Estates General an influence *equal* to that of the privileged. I repeat, can the Third demand any less? And is it not clear that if its influence is less than equal it cannot hope to escape from its political nonexistence and become *something?*

But what is really unfortunate is that the three articles of the Third Estate's claim are not sufficient to give it the equality of influence that it cannot in fact do without. In vain will it get an equal number of representatives drawn from its order: the influence of the privileged will infiltrate and dominate even within the sanctuary of the Third. Who has the offices, the employment, the patronage to give? On which side is there need for protection? Which side has the power to protect? . . . And the nonprivileged who would seem from their talents to be the most suitable to uphold the interests of their order, are they not from childhood indoctrinated with a superstitious or compulsory respect for the nobility? It is well known how easy it is for men in general to submit to all the practices that can be useful to them. They think constantly of bettering their lot; and when personal industriousness does not advance them by honest means it impels them into false ways. Some ancient people or other, in order to accustom their children to violent or dexterous exercises, withheld food until they had succeeded or made an effort. In the same way, among us, the most capable class of the Third Estate has been forced, in order to obtain the necessities, to devote itself to the purposes of the powerful. This part of the nation has thereby come to compose something like a great antechamber where, occupied ceaselessly with what its masters say or do, it is always ready to sacrifice everything for the advantages it hopes to gain from the good fortune of pleasing them. . . .

In addition to the power of the aristocracy, which in France controls everything, and of that feudal superstition that still degrades most people's minds, there is the influence of property: this is natural; I do not reject it; but one must agree that it is still completely to the advantage of the privileged and that there is good reason to fear that they will benefit from its powerful support at the expense of the Third Estate. . . .

The First Demand

[The Third Estate demands] that the representatives of the Third Estate be chosen only from among citizens who really belong to the Third.

We have already explained that in order to belong to the Third in actuality it is necessary not to have been tarnished by any kind of privilege. . . .

It is argued, in addition, that to restrict the free choice of the voters is damaging to their liberty; I have two replies to make to this alleged difficulty. . . . Without doubt, the constituents must be left their entire liberty, and it is for that very reason that it is necessary to exclude from their number all the privileged, who are too much accustomed to dominating the people overbearingly.

My second reply is straightforward. You cannot have, in any fashion, a liberty or a right without limits. In all countries, the law has fixed upon certain characteristics without which one can be neither a voter nor eligible for office. Thus, for example, the law must determine the age below which one will be considered unsuitable for representing one's fellow citizens. Similarly women everywhere, for better or worse, are kept from this sort of representation. It is an established fact that a vagabond, a beggar, cannot be charged with the political mandate of the people. Would a servant or anyone dependent upon a master, or an unnaturalized alien, be allowed to appear among the nation's representatives? Thus political liberty, like civil liberty, has its limits. It is only a question of knowing whether the condition of noneligibility upon which the Third insists is as essential as all those that I have just indicated. Now the comparison is entirely in its favor; for a beggar, an alien, can be without any interest opposed to the interest of the Third. Whereas the noble and the ecclesiastic are in the nature of things partisans of the privileges from which they profit. . . .

As a result of these principles, members of the Third Estate who are too closely connected with the members of the first two orders must not be entrusted with the confidence of the commoners. . . . I demand especially that attention be given to the numerous agents of feudality.

It is to the odious remains of this barbarous regime that we owe the division that still exists, unfortunately for France, among three orders hostile to each other. All would be lost if the mandatories of feudalism were able to usurp the function of representing the commoners.

In the eyes of some, the argument that we have just refuted was rescued by the observation that the Third Estate lacked members with enough enlightenment, courage, and so on, to represent it, and that it was necessary to seek help from the nobility. . . . This strange assertion does not merit an answer. Consider the classes *available* within the Third Estate—and like everyone else I mean by available classes those with sufficient wealth to receive a liberal education, cultivate their reason, and take an interest in public affairs. Those classes have no other interest than that of the rest of the people. See if they do not contain enough citizens who are ed-

Bourgeoisie Desires

By and large . . . the bourgeoisie hotly resented their inferior social status. . . . They longed for an order of society in which money, not birth, would be the controlling consideration. They desired greater scope for personal initiative and enterprise, the elimination of state interference with the free play of economic forces. They were keenly interested in attaining a fuller measure of happiness on this earth.

Ambitious, hard-working, self-assured, the French bourgeoisie greedily devoured the publications of the *philosophes* which so engagingly expressed what the middle classes thought. Books forbidden by the censorship were "bootlegged" about with remarkable abandon, and their contents were discussed in homes, societies, clubs and lodges. Men of the middle classes came confidently to believe that the future belonged to them. The French Revolution would be a bourgeois movement in the main; and the minds and emotions of the middle classes were prepared for significant changes before they made them the work of their hands.

Arthur J. May, *A History of Civilization*, 1964.

ucated, honest, and worthy in every way to be good representatives of the nation. . . .

The Second Demand

[The Third Estate demands] that its deputies be equal in number to those of the two privileged orders.

. . . Political rights, like civil rights, must be attached to the quality of citizen. This legal property is the same for all without regard to the greater or lesser amount of real property composing the fortune or possession of each individual. Every citizen who fulfills the conditions determined for electors has a right to be represented, and his representation cannot be a fraction of the representation of another. This right is unitary; all exercise it equally, just as all are equally protected by the law to whose making they have contributed. How can it be maintained, on the one hand, that the law is the expression of the general will, in other words of the plurality, and claimed at the same time that ten individual wills can balance a thousand particular wills? Does this not leave the way open to lawmaking by the minority, which is obviously contrary to the nature of things? . . .

In terms of population, it is well known what a great superiority the third order has over the first two. No more than anyone else do I know the exact relationship, but like everyone I will allow myself to make an estimate. . . .

Thus in all there are somewhat less than two hundred thousand privileged of the first two orders. Compare this number to twenty-five or twenty-six million and judge for yourself. . . .

In the days of Philip the Fair,[2] a few good towns sufficed to provide for a chamber for commoners in the Estates General.

Since that time, feudal servitude has disappeared and the countryside has produced a numerous population of *new citizens.* Cities have grown in numbers and size. . . .

Think of how the former relationship of the orders to each other has changed from two sides at once; the Third, which had been reduced to nothing, has reacquired through its industry a portion of what the abuses of the stronger had taken from it. Instead of

2. Philip IV, king of France from 1285 to 1314

demanding the return of its rights, it has consented to pay for them; they have not been restored to the Third, but sold back to it. But finally, in one way or another, it can take possession of them. It must not be ignorant of the fact that today it is the national reality whereas it used to be only the shadow; that during this long transformation the nobility has ceased to be the monstrous feudal reality that could oppress with impunity and is now its mere shadow, and that in vain this shadow still seeks to frighten an entire nation.

The Third and Last Demand

[The Third Estate demands] that the Estates General vote not by orders but by head.

. . . There are surely abuses in France; these abuses benefit someone: it is scarcely the Third Estate to which they are advantageous, but it is certainly the Third to which they are harmful. Now I ask whether, given this state of affairs, it is possible to destroy any abuse as long as the *veto* is left in the hands of those who profit from it. All justice would be powerless; everything would have to wait upon the pure generosity of the privileged. Would that be what one thinks of as social order? . . . But could the three orders as they are now constituted join together to vote by head? That is the real question. No. According to true principles, they cannot vote *in common* either by head or by orders. Whatever proportion you adopt among them, it cannot fulfill the objective that is proposed, which would be to link together the totality of representatives by *one* common will. No doubt this assertion needs development and proofs. . . .

The time is past when the three orders, thinking only of defending themselves against ministerial despotism, were ready to join forces against the common enemy. Although it is impossible for the nation to profit from the present circumstances or to take a single step toward an improved social order without the Third Estate sharing in the benefits, nevertheless the pride of the two higher orders is irritated at seeing the great municipalities of the kingdom demand even the smallest part of the political rights that belong to the people. What did they want, then, these privileged who are so ardent to defend their superabundance, so prompt to prevent the Third Estate from obtaining the merest necessities of this kind? Did they mean for the regeneration of which they are so proud to be only for themselves? And did they wish to use the always unfortunate people only as a blind instrument for the extension and consecration of their aristocracy? . . .

In vain the Third Estate expected the collaboration of all classes to restore its political rights and the fullness of its civil rights; fear of seeing the abuses reformed inspires in the first two orders an alarm that outweighs their desire for liberty. Between liberty and a few odious privileges, they have chosen the latter. In their hearts they have discovered an affinity for the favors of servitude. Today they fear those very Estates General for which they called not long ago with so much ardor. . . .

The Third Estate's Only Choice

For the Third Estate, moreover, it is no longer a question of being better off or remaining as it was. Circumstances no longer permit this choice; it is now a case of advancing or losing ground; of either abolishing or recognizing and legalizing iniquitous and antisocial privileges. Now it must be obvious how senseless it would be to consecrate, at the end of the eighteenth century, the abominable remains of feudalism.

Viewpoint 5

"[The peasants] stagnate, living in misery, crushed beneath the entire weight of the most inhumane and detestable feudal system."

The Peasants Sought Greater Economic Freedoms

Inhabitants of Montjoye-Vaufrey

The French economy in the eighteenth century was based heavily on the feudal system, in which a feudal lord or *seigneur* owned large swaths of land on which peasants worked in exchange for portions of the crops. Peasants became increasingly disillusioned with the feudal system in the 1780s. In the following viewpoint, taken from a *cahier* (letter) written to finance minister Jacque Necker by the inhabitants of the feudal lands in Montjoye-Vaufrey, the peasants argue that their seigneur has exploited them economically. According to the peasants, the feudal lord demands excessive tithes, wrongfully appropriates communal lands, and compels his workers to cater to his whims. The feudal system was abolished on August 4, 1789.

Inhabitants of Montjoye-Vaufrey, "Cahiers from Rural Districts: Attack on Seigneurial Dues," 1789.

[T]his is a] statement concerning the unjust, onerous, and humiliating dues and other unheard of burdens which the undersigned inhabitants of the seigneury [feudal lands] of Montjoye-Vaufrey are made to endure by the Count of Montjoye-Vaufrey. The seigneury of Montjoye-Vaufrey is small with almost inaccessible mountains, covered in large part by forests of beech and fir trees. The soil is naturally barren and produces nothing but brambles and thorn bushes. It is part of Upper Alsace and enclosed by the diocese of Basle, lying on the kingdom's border. Close to one thousand individuals live in this region, which is almost wild because of its location. There they stagnate, living in misery, crushed beneath the entire weight of the most inhumane and detestable feudal system and the victims of the thousands of abuses that the seigneur [feudal lord] of Montjoye heaps upon them. The truth of these statements will be found to be more than convincing once we have outlined the rights that the [seigneur] claims to have over them and the manner in which these rights are exercised.

Unfair Tithes

The Tithe of the Sixth Sheaf

The seigneur demands one of every six sheaves produced on the majority of the lands of the seigneury. The other sheaves are left to the owner, who uses one and a half sheaves for seed because the soil only yields four sheaves for every sheaf planted. The remaining three and a half sheaves constitute his only profit from sowing and are used to feed himself and to pay other seigneurial dues.

The Right of Mortmain

The same lands on which the seigneur collects this unusual tithe are also subject to mortmain [death duty], and he exercises this right with such cruelty that the poor unfortunate owner cannot sell his land, even when reduced to a state of destitution deserving of the greatest compassion. We have seen infirm persons, possessing land, but forbidden to sell it by the seigneur, who are led by their charitable fellow-citizens from village to village begging for alms. Gardens, houses, and orchards were once exempt from this duty, but today he takes everything in case the owner dies without an heir.

Corvées

It would seem that the owners of these same lands should be left

In 1780, French peasants, increasingly disillusioned with the feudal system, began to protest their exploitation.

to enjoy their produce in peace, obliged as they are to submit to such an outrageous tithe and to the odious exercise of the right of mortmain. But far from it. In addition, this seigneur requires five days of work from them, and if he obliges them to perform this service in actual labor, he assigns the work when it is convenient for him. It is often the case that those subject to the corvée are not able to fulfill their tasks in a day, whereupon they are obliged to continue their work the next day, even though only one day of work is counted. If he does not require actual labor from them, someone who has two oxen is forced to pay him six livres. . . . Some people have preferred to endure this additional charge rather than to provide the actual labor, but the worker with no beasts of burden performs the corvée with his own hands. Or, if he wants to commute his work into money, he is forced to pay three livres fifteen sols, whereas before he would only have paid thirty-three sols. Poor beggars are not exempt. They are seen going from door to door asking for bread in order to go and work for the seigneur, because recently he refuses all food to those required to work at the corvée.

Taxes, Hens, the Sale of Wine, Residence Rights

For each journal of land [a measure of land equal to the amount a plowman could plow in a day] he takes eight deniers in taxes, three hens for each hearth, and the poor are no more exempt than the richest inhabitant. He collects a tenth of the wine sold in inns, whereas the king only takes a twentieth. He makes each person who moves to a new community pay a florin a year for this right. Outsiders are also subject to this payment.

Controlling the Land

Withholding Right

For approximately ten years, he has assumed a withholding right with respect to most of the land sold in the seigneury. He sells this right to whomever he wants; therefore the heir can be banished from the land. The rights of family are held in just as much contempt as those of humanity.

The Bread Riots

In addition to hatred of the feudal system, one reason why peasants revolted against the "old regime" of France was because of rising bread prices. In the following excerpt from his book The Crowd in the French Revolution, *George Rudé notes that this economic concern often placed France's poor at odds with the middle class.*

The most constant motive of popular insurrection during the Revolution, as in the eighteenth century as a whole, was the compelling need of the *menu peuple* [the common people] for the provision of cheap and plentiful bread and other essentials, and the necessary administrative measures to ensure it. . . . This preoccupation, being at variance with the ideas on free trade and property held by all *bourgeois* [middle-class] groups, was apt to put a strain on their alliance with even the most advanced of the political leaders. It would, of course, have been comforting for the journalists of the Palais Royal and the deputies and orators of the revolutionary Assemblies and Jacobin Club [a group of radical revolutionaries] if the common

Communal Forests
His greed leads him to appropriate all of the communal forests, selling them for his own profit. This usurpation has already been seen in the communities of Montjoye, Monnoiront, and Les Choseaux. He gives them to whomever he pleases. The distribution is never in proportion to the needs of the individual, demonstrating his absolute mastery. However, individuals pay royal taxes and even the subsidy, a tax which in Alsace is particularly heavy on forests.

Communal Pasturelands
The same observations can be made with regard to communal pasturelands. The seigneur does not allow land to be cleared at all unless one agrees to plant and give him a sixth of what is produced. Otherwise it is forbidden to touch the smallest bramble or

---

people of the markets and *faubourgs* [urban areas where the poor lived] had been content to bedeck themselves with tricolour cockades and *bonnets rouges* [red caps] and to mouth patriotic-radical slogans without concerning themselves overmuch with the satisfaction of their own particular needs and grievances—if the Réveillon rioters, for example, had not insisted on accompanying their shouting of the unexceptionable slogan of 'Vive le Tiers État!' ["Long live the Third Estate," the Third Estate being all of France except the nobles and clergy] with the destruction of the properties of such stalwarts of the official Third Estate as Henriot and Réveillon[1]; or if the women of the markets had been merely satisfied to march to Versailles to fetch the royal family to Paris—as required by the constitutional monarchists—without agitating so violently and vociferously for more bread and better quality flour.

1. Henriot and Réveillon were two Parisian manufacturers whose comments linking reduced bread prices to lower wages led to deadly riots on April 27 and 28, 1789.

George Rudé, *The Crowd in the French Revolution*, 1959.

thorn. Sometimes he seizes certain portions of these pasturelands that meet his needs, and at other times he cedes them to different individuals.

Beating the Woods

Nothing demonstrates the slavery in which he holds these unfortunate people, and the odious use that he makes of his power, more than their obligation to cater to his whims. When it pleases him, and as often as it pleases him, he obliges them to beat the woods in order to satisfy his desire to hunt. As he does all of the others, he exercises the right arbitrarily. The farmer who is thus forced to wander through the woods for a whole day receives neither sustenance, nor a bonus, nor payment. If he refuses to do this work, the seigneur levies a fine to compensate for his loss of recreation, and his judge never fails to rule in favor of the plaintiff. . . .

For more than a century, they have taken their seigneur to court in order to oblige him to produce the legal titles which give him the right to oppress them. To thwart these just measures, the predecessors of the current seigneur had the deputies of the leading communities clapped in irons and imprisoned, charging them with insubordination and holding them in custody at the seigneur's will. The current seigneur has again outdone his predecessors. For two months, he has kept . . . an entire family composed of six heads of household in prison, and he has charged each fifteen gold louis. He has had several others imprisoned. This kind of violence holds all of these unfortunate people in the cruelest fear and slavery. Until now, each imprisonment has been the signal for the creation of a new tax, and it is in this very unusual manner that he perpetuates these different humiliations and creates new ones.

Viewpoint 6

"Throughout the seventeenth and eighteenth centuries [financial difficulties] were the normal state of affairs."

The French Monarchy Was Beset with Financial Problems

William Doyle

In the following viewpoint William Doyle details the financial difficulties that crippled the French monarchy and inevitably led to revolution. According to Doyle, the deficit had risen steadily since 1777, with much of the debt the result of excessive military spending. He examines the suggestions made by Louis XVI's comptroller-general, Charles Alexander Calonne, to solve France's financial problems, including reducing spending, raising taxes, and declaring bankruptcy. As explained by Doyle, Calonne concluded that only a complete reform of the monarchy would end the financial crisis. Doyle is the chairman of the School of History at the University of Bristol in England.

William Doyle, *Origins of the French Revolution*. Oxford, UK: Oxford University Press, 1988. Copyright © 1980 by William Doyle. Reproduced by permission of the publisher.

The revolution that was to sweep away the political institutions of old France, and shake her society to its foundations, did not begin on 14 July 1789. By that time the old order was already in ruins, beyond reconstruction. This was the result of a chain of events that can be traced as far back as 20 August 1786. For it was on that day that [Charles Alexander] Calonne, comptroller-general of the royal finances, first came to Louis XVI and informed him that the state was on the brink of financial collapse.

We have no absolutely reliable or completely unambiguous figures to illustrate the financial condition of France in 1786. Nor did contemporaries have such figures. Even Calonne, with all the accounts of the royal treasury at his disposal, claimed that it had taken him two years to arrive at his own assessment of the problem. But the seriousness of the situation was beyond dispute. According to Calonne, the total revenue for 1786 would amount to 475 million *livres*, but expenditure would probably total 587 millions—a deficit of 112 millions, or almost a quarter of the annual revenue. When Louis XVI had come to the throne in 1774, Calonne claimed, the deficit had been 40 millions, and it had even fallen over the next two years. But since 1777 it had risen steadily, and there was every prospect, over the next few years, of its rising further if drastic action was not soon taken. The basic reason for this deterioration was that since 1777 there had been an enormous rise in state borrowing and consequently in the annual interest and repayments that the treasury was obliged to disburse. Since 1776, Calonne claimed, 1,250 millions had been borrowed. Until 1794, 50 millions per year of short-term loans would fall due for repayment, and meanwhile, the cost of servicing the total debt ate up nearly half of the annual revenue. Worse still, no less than 280 millions of the next year's revenues had already been anticipated in order to raise money for earlier expenditure.

A Long History of Financial Problems

Financial difficulties were nothing new under the French monarchy. Indeed, throughout the seventeenth and eighteenth centuries they were the normal state of affairs; it was the rare moments of financial health that were extraordinary. Nor was the cause of these difficulties any mystery. Successive kings had always spent too much on war. The wars of Louis XIV had imposed a crippling legacy of debt on the royal finances, and although this burden was much alleviated by the great financial crash of 1720–21, which enabled the government to write off huge sums, four major European and overseas wars since that time had brought matters once more to crisis proportions. They were already serious by 1763, at the end of seven years of costly and unsuccessful conflict on a worldwide scale; the deficit had reached 50 millions, and for the next fifteen years successive comptrollers-general of the finances warned unceasingly against the dangers of further wars. French participation in the American War of Independence between 1778 and 1783 was glorious and successful, but it confirmed these ministers' worst fears. By 1783, the financial situation was as bad as it had been in 1715, and over the next three years it continued to deteriorate to the point which Calonne announced to the king in August 1786.

Evaluating the Remedies

A number of obvious expedients are open to governments in financial difficulties. Unfortunately, most of these expedients were not open to Calonne—or, if they were, there were reasons why they could not prove as effective as they should.

One natural step, for example, was to effect economies [i.e., reduce spending]. There was undoubtedly scope for this, and the plan which Calonne put forward to the Assembly of Notables[1] the next year was to include a number of money-saving proposals. Nevertheless, none of the major items of public expenditure could be substantially reduced. . . . The armed forces could only be markedly reduced at the cost of jeopardizing France's international position at a moment when the internal instability of the Dutch Republic and uncertainties in Eastern Europe following the death of Frederick the Great made the international situation ominous. Economies, therefore, must largely be a matter of trimming expenditure over a whole range of minor items such as pensions, the royal household, public works, and welfare services

1. The Assembly of Notables was a collection of nobles and other elites convened by Louis XVI in August 1786.

which together accounted for only about one-seventh of annual outlay . . . nowhere near enough to meet a deficit on the scale of 1786. Clearly economies could only be effective in conjunction with more comprehensive measures.

A second possibility would be to increase taxes. Yet France was already one of the most highly taxed nations in Europe. It is true that the average Dutchman or Englishman paid more per head in taxes than his French counterpart; but in France there were immense regional diversities, so that taxpayers in the Paris region paid more per head than anybody else in Europe. And when we consider that the populations of Great Britain and the Dutch Republic were in any case far wealthier as a whole than that of France, the French burden appears all the greater. What is more, it seemed to have increased inordinately within living memory. . . . In 1749, a new tax on landed property of 5 per cent had been introduced—the *vingtième*. It proved to be permanent. In 1756, it had been doubled for a limited period, but in practice the government never felt able to do without the extra revenue, so this second *vingtième* became in effect as permanent as the first. Between 1760 and 1763, the most costly period of the Seven Years War, a third *vingtième* was levied; and in 1783, it was reintroduced with the assurance that it would end three years after peace was concluded. That moment came at the end of 1786, and this imminent fall in revenue was another of the factors which led Calonne to confront the crisis when he did. . . .

Another possibility was for the state simply to renounce its overwhelming burden of debt by declaring bankruptcy. Earlier governments had often adopted this expedient; but over the eighteenth century it had come to seem less and less respectable. The financial crash of 1720, in which thousands of government creditors were ruined, and a series of reductions in the *rentes* (government annuities) in the chaotic years following that crisis, had instilled French public opinion with a deep hostility to breaches of public faith, and from 1726 onwards governments had striven to keep public confidence by avoiding any suggestion that they might default on their debts. . . . The lesson seemed clear; bankruptcy was not only dishonourable, it destroyed the state's credit and made further borrowing difficult. . . . [Anne-Robert]

Turgot, and every minister who followed him, Calonne included, set their faces firmly against even partial bankruptcy. The determination of successive revolutionary assemblies down to 1797 to honour the debts accumulated under the old order shows how deeply and generally public opinion shared the view that the public debt should be sacrosanct.

But Calonne could hardly go on borrowing. It is true that the plan of action which he laid before the king contained proposals for further loans in order to cover the repayments of the coming years, but there was no long-term future in fighting a debt problem by new borrowings. In any case it was uncertain whether such borrowing would even be possible. The French government already borrowed money on terms distinctly less favourable than either the British or the Dutch, because in France there was no publicly supported bank through which government credit could be cheaply channelled. . . . In the absence of a bank, the government was compelled to rely on intermediaries for raising its loans, bodies like the municipality of Paris, the estates of provinces that retained them (like Languedoc and Brittany), or great corporations like the clergy, all of which could borrow money on better terms than the king. But when needs were extraordinary even these resources were not enough. Then, the government was compelled to float loans on its own behalf, but on terms so generous that even the most prudent investor found them hard to resist. This is what happened between 1777 and 1786. . . .

An expedient that Calonne did not consider was a reform of the system by which the government financed its activities. One reason why it took him so long to come to any conclusions about the true state of the finances was that the king had no central treasury where accounts were kept, revenues taken in, and payments made. Nor was there any real notion of an annual budget. Most of the state's finances were handled by independent financiers who had bought the right to handle government revenues, either through membership of the company of Farmers-General, who collected most of the indirect taxes, or through buying an office of accountant (variously called payers, receivers, or treasurers) to a government department. Once in office, all that these officials were obliged to do was to receive or pay out funds on the government's orders, and send in periodic accounts to the crown's courts of audit, the *chambres des comptes*. What they did with the money in their accounts otherwise was their own affair. And what they often did with it in practice was to lend it to the government in short-term credits—so that the king found himself borrowing and paying interest on his own money. The day-to-day payments of the government, in fact, depended on short-term credits of this sort, the *anticipations* which ate up so much of the expected revenue for 1787, advanced by men who were nominally state employees, but who in reality were private businessmen making a profit from manipulating public funds. Nor did such businessmen confine their activities to juggling with the state's money. They normally had extensive private financial dealings, too, and made no distinction between the two fields of activity. So that when, in times of economic stringency, their operations came under strain, so did the finances of the government. This is what happened in 1770 and again in 1786–87, when the government's difficulties were heralded by the bankruptcy of a number of its financiers. A state bank would, of course, have freed the government from its dependence on these profiteering agents, who constituted in effect a body of several hundred petty bankers. . . .

Reforming the Economy, Government, and Society

With so many courses of action either closed or considered impractical, what then did Calonne propose to do in order to resolve the crisis? Nothing could put it more clearly than his own words. 'I shall easily show,' he declared to the king, 'that it is impossible to tax further, ruinous to be always borrowing and not enough to confine ourselves to economical reforms and that, with matters as they are, ordinary ways being unable to lead us to our goal, the only effective remedy, the only course left to take, the only means of managing finally to put the finances truly in order, must consist in revivifying the entire State by recasting all that is vicious in its constitution.' He was proposing something quite unprecedented in the history of the monarchy—a total and comprehensive reform of all its institutions, according to clear principles, in such a way that it should never fall into difficulties like those of the 1780s again.

In the document he presented to the king, *Summary of a Plan for the Improvement of the Finances*, Calonne never defined his guiding principle in a few words. But it emerged very clearly from the way he put the problem. . . . In short, the French state lacked rational organization and uniform principles, and it was not enough to attempt to solve financial problems, as previous ministries had, by exclusively financial means. Calonne believed that it was now necessary to reform the economy, government, and to some degree French society itself.

Viewpoint 7

"It was the domestic perception of financial problems, not their reality, that propelled successive French governments from anxiety to alarm to outright panic."

The French Monarchy's Financial Problems Were Exaggerated

Simon Schama

In the following viewpoint Simon Schama argues that the financial difficulties France experienced in the 1770s and 1780s were not a primary cause of the revolution. According to Schama it was the perception, not the reality, of irreparable economic problems that caused anxiety and unrest. He contends that although the various wars France fought during the eighteenth century created substantial debts, those debts were no worse than those of other European nations. Schama is a professor of history at Columbia University in New York City and the author of *Citizens: A Chronicle of the French Revolution*, the source of the following viewpoint.

If the causes of the French Revolution are complex, the causes of the downfall of the monarchy are not. The two phenomena are not identical, since the end of absolutism in France did not of itself entail a revolution of such transformative power as actually came to pass in France. But the end of the old regime was the necessary condition of the beginning of a new, and that was brought about, in the first instance, by a cash-flow crisis. It was the politicization of the money crisis that dictated the calling of the Estates-General.[1]

A Pyrrhic Military Victory

To do them justice, the ministers of Louis XVI were painfully impaled on the horns of a dilemma. It was quite reasonable for them to wish to restore France's position in the Atlantic since they correctly saw that it was in the sugar islands of the Caribbean and the potential markets of the Anglophone colonies that the greatest fortunes were being made. In this sense, prudent economic strategy demanded a policy of intervention on the side of the Americans. Both during the war and after the peace of 1783 official statements defended that intervention as designed not to annex imperial possessions but rather to secure freedom of commerce. And it was in that guise—as the protector of free navigation—that Louis XVI appears on most celebratory engravings. There can be no doubt that in the short run these aims were accomplished, for Atlantic trade from Nantes and Bordeaux to the French West Indies reached an unprecedented height of prosperity in the decade before the Revolution. In this sense, military investment in the spoils of empire had paid off handsomely.

The financial consequences of that same policy, however, made it a pyrrhic victory. For the ballooning of the deficit so weakened the *nerfs*—the sinews—of state that by 1787, its foreign policy was robbed of real freedom of action. For in that year sheer financial exigency prevented France from intervening decisively in the civil war in the Dutch Republic to support its own partisans, themselves going by the name of "Patriots." Paradoxically, then, the war that had been intended to restore the imperial power of France ended up compromising it so badly that king and *patrie*

1. a legislative assembly that existed prior to the Revolution

[fatherland] seemed to be two different, and before long irreconcilable, entities. It was not much longer before this process was taken even further, so that the court itself seemed a foreign parasite feeding off the body of the "true" Nation.

It needs to be stressed that it was policies—fiscal and political as well as military—that brought the monarchy to its knees. Excessively influenced by the obsolescence implied by the nomenclature of the *ancien régime*[2] (a term not used until 1790 and then, in [Honoré] Mirabeau's letter to the King, meaning "previous" not "archaic"), historians have been accustomed to tracing the sources of France's financial predicament to the structure of its institutions, rather than to particular decisions taken by its governments. Heavy emphasis on both institutional and social history at the expense of politics has reinforced the impression of administrations hopelessly trapped inside a system that, some day or other, would be doomed to collapse under the strain of its own contradictions.

As we shall see, nothing of the sort was true. What, seen from the vantage point of the Revolution, might look incorrigibly inflexible was in fact open to a number of approaches in coping with French financial problems. The trouble lay rather in the political difficulties in sustaining those policy decisions to the point where they might have paid off, and in the repeated retreats of the King to what he judged was the temporarily least painful political alternative. If anything, as [Alexis] de Tocqueville pointed out, it was not an aversion to reform but an obsession with it that made consistent financial management difficult if not impossible. Where de Tocqueville erred, though, was in supposing that French institutions were themselves intrinsically incapable of solving the regime's fiscal problems. In this view, there were no short-term problems, only deep-seated structural ones that could not be changed—*even by the Revolution*—for he thought he saw the same ills of centralization and the heavy hand of bureaucratic despotism recurring endlessly and hopelessly through French history.

How grave was France's financial predicament after the American war? It had, it is true, run up an imposing debt, but one that was no worse than comparable debts incurred in fighting the other

2. The name given to France's pre-revolutionary government.

wars deemed equally essential to sustain the nation's position as a great power. Those quick to condemn the ministers of Louis XVI for their hopeless prodigality might pause to reflect that no state with imperial pretensions has, in fact, ever subordinated what it takes to be irreducible military interests to the considerations of a balanced budget. And like apologists for powerful military force in twentieth-century America and the Soviet Union, advocates of similar "indispensable" resources in eighteenth-century France pointed to the country's vast demographic and economic reserves and a flourishing economy to sustain the burden. Indeed the prospering of that economy was, they claimed, contingent on such military expenditure, both directly in naval bases like Brest and Toulon, and indirectly in the protection it gave to the most rapidly expanding sector of the economy.

Moreover, on each occasion following the wars of the eighteenth century, there had been a period of painful but necessary adjustment to allow the finances of the realm to be brought into manageable order once more. The wretched end to Louis XIV's wars, for example, saw simultaneously the specter of bankruptcy, the virtual disintegration of the French army in the field, tax revolts and mass famine. And by 1714 the debt was calculated at around 2.6 billion livres *tournois* or, in a population of twenty-three million, 113 livres—about two-thirds the annual income of a master carpenter or tailor—for each subject of the Sun King. In the sobering aftermath, there was an attempt to learn from the "victorious" Anglo-Dutch side by importing their banking principles into French public finance. An enterprising Scotsman, John Law, was given the opportunity to manage and eventually liquidate the French debt in return for exclusive license to a newly created Bank of France. Unhappily, Law used the capital subscribed to the Bank to speculate in phantom American land companies and when the inflated bubble burst, so did the principle of a Bank-managed national deficit. In fact, Law's speculations were no more outrageous or indeed reprehensible than identical gambling by the South Sea Company in Britain. But the principle of a public Bank survived the debacle better there because such financial institutions were transferred more strictly to parliamentary control. In France, there was no comparable institution that could act as a dependable watchdog and so reassure future depositors and creditors of the government. It has been well said by Michel Morineau that the difference between the two debts is that the French deficit was burdened by being broadly conceived by the public as "royal" while the British debt was held to be "national."

Short of a Bank-managed loan system, there were still financial strategies open to French governments to keep their debt at a manageable level. Controllers-General of the period of the Regency following Louis XIV's death indulged in a drastic writing-down of the scale of debt and intervened radically in redemption schedules. This was, to be sure, a kind of bankruptcy by installments but, perhaps surprisingly, it did not seriously impair the future credit of the French crown. As long as there was capital, both within and outside the country, looking for yields that were even marginally higher than other kinds of domestic investment, France did not lack for lenders. By 1726 the French budget was more or less in balance, and with the help of inflation reducing the real value of the debt, the nation's finances even survived the War of Polish Partition in the 1730s without excessive new burdens.

It was quite otherwise, however, with the two major wars that then followed: the War of Austrian Succession from 1740 to 1748 and, still more spectacularly, the Seven Years' War from 1756 to 1763. The first conflict, essentially on land, cost around 1 billion livres and the second, both a naval and land war, 1.8 billion. By 1753 the principal of the deficit had shot up to 1.2 billion and annual interest to 85 million livres, already 20 percent of current revenue. Yet the postwar Controller-General Machault d'Arnouville projected that the deficit might be paid off within fifty to sixty years, assuming no further wars. That was, of course, like assuming there would be no France or, more seriously, no Britain. After the next war, in 1764, the deficit was up to 2.324 billion livres in principal with debt service alone taking something like 60 percent of the budget, or twice the proportion of the 1750s. In thirteen years the debt had grown by 1 billion livres.

Why Economics Led to a Revolution

While this makes grim (if familiar) reading for accountants, it did not of itself set France on a trajectory to revolution. The mid-eighteenth century had witnessed an enormous expansion, both quantitative and qualitative, in the scale and sophistication of warfare, which had taken a heavy toll of all major belligerent powers. Hohenzollern Prussia,[3] which we are accustomed to think of as a success story of bureaucratic militarism, was in a desperate plight at the end of the Seven Years' War even though it had been kept afloat by British subsidies. Its remedy for ills was in fact to import the *French* system of tax management: the *régie*, which actually returned it to some degree of fiscal soundness. Not even neutrals escaped, for the Dutch Republic, which itself had been busy funding any and all customers, went into serious depression in 1763–64. And Britain, held up as the other major example of fiscal competence, went into debt (as it would during the American war) on precisely the same scale and magnitude as its archenemy. Not only do we now know that the British per capita tax burden was *three times* heavier than in France, but by 1782, the percentage of public revenue consumed to service Britain's debt—on the order of 70 percent—was also considerably greater than the French equivalent.

So in absolute terms, even after the immense fiscal havoc wrought by the American war, there are few grounds for seeing the scale of the French deficit as *necessarily* leading to catastrophe. But it was the domestic perception of financial problems, not their reality, that propelled successive French governments from anxiety to alarm to outright panic. The determining elements in the money crisis of the French state, then, were all political and psychological, not institutional or fiscal. . . .

No Competent Bureaucracies

For a long time now, historians have argued that what ministers of the French crown did or didn't do about the debt is of minor importance. For it was the nature of the old-regime monarchy itself that was the real problem. Hamstrung by privilege, how could a government consisting of men who bought or inherited their offices hope for even a modicum of bureaucratic efficiency? Even with the best will in the world, and with able public servants (nei-

3. The Hohenzollern family were the dominant political family in Germany from 1415 to 1918. They ruled Prussia from 1701 to 1918.

ther of which could be counted on), French government was a vacuum presiding over a chaos. Add to this its monstrous deficit, and the wonder is not that it ended badly, but that it survived as long as it did.

But is this argument valid? It assumes, to begin with, that to work adequately, the eighteenth-century state should have approximated some early version of "civil service" government. This might be defined as a polity in which public functions are the monopoly of salaried officials, trained for the bureaucracy, hired by merit, disentangled from any private interest in the jurisdiction they serve and accountable to some sort of disinterested sovereign body. It is true enough that the outlines of such a bureaucratic mechanism were articulated in the eighteenth-century "science" of "cameral government" and that, for the first time, professors of such *Kameral-und-polizeiwissenschaft*—what we would call government and finance—were occupying specially created chairs at universities, especially in the German-speaking world. But it takes no more than a glance at the reality of eighteenth-century government throughout Europe to see that these principles were most honored in the breach. The celebrated Prussian bureaucracy, for example, was riddled with corruption, was the creature of dynasties of nobles who settled in swarms on its offices. And in that state, local government officers were appointed not for their separation from, but adhesion to the local society of landowners. By comparison the French *intendants*[4] were models of integrity and objectivity. Even in Britain, Hanoverian government was notorious for sinecures created to generate chains of political loyalty. I don't mean to suggest that bureaucratic competence was not possible within such a system, but the same holds true for French government as much as any other. . . .

Reckless but Not Obtuse

So just how serious were the results of the eighteenth-century monarchy's combination of business and bureaucracy in managing its own finances? For a long time it has been said that the

4. Intendants were the main agents of the crown in the provinces under the Old Regime.

messiness of these arrangements, for example, delayed the appearance of a systematic budget until [finance minister Jacques] Necker tried to provide his own published one in 1781. But as Michel Morineau, in a superlative study of these issues, has shown, while there was no public record, there certainly were *arrangements* that enabled Controllers-General both to apportion expenses among departments of state and to see with fairly reliable accuracy how much money was actually disbursed to those departments. And historians have been equally certain that had the monarchy had the courage to assume directly the business of administering and collecting indirect taxes, it would have saved the admittedly enormous profits going to the commercial "middlemen" who did the taxing on its behalf. On the other hand, however, it would have been saddled with those extra costs of administration, which might well have offset the gains, not to mention the odium which inescapably went with the collection of taxes on basic commodities. It has been estimated that the "overheads" of French revenue collection amounted to 13 percent of the total, compared with 10 percent in the case of Britain, where a centralized bureaucracy did indeed run the customs and excises. If this is really all that was at stake, no wonder Controllers-General were reluctant to upset their habitual regime for some sort of theoretical sovereignty over public business.

It was the policies of the old regime rather than its operational structure that brought it close to bankruptcy and political disaster. Compared with the consequences that flowed from the great decisions of foreign policy, privilege, venality and indirect administration of revenue were of much less significance. At the root of its problems was the cost of armaments when coupled with political resistance to new taxes and a growing willingness of governments to accept high interest-bearing obligations from both domestic and, increasingly, foreign creditors. No doubt it was reckless of French governments in the 1780s to lay up so much trouble for themselves. But it takes a very superior form of hindsight on the part of an American in the 1980s to write them off as hopelessly obtuse.

CHAPTER 2

The Controversial Events of the French Revolution

Chapter Preface

L ouis XVI was a man who should never have become king. His grandfather was Louis XV, who ruled France from 1715 to 1774. Under normal circumstances the younger man would have remained a prince, but the untimely deaths of his father and two older brothers left the twenty-year-old in charge of a troubled nation. Economic problems had begun to beset France during Louis XV's reign, setting the stage for the French Revolution, which started fifteen years into Louis XVI's reign. On January 21, 1793, three and a half years after the storming of the Bastille (a prison and fortress in Paris), the king was beheaded. His death was the ultimate symbol of the revolutionary government's decision to transform France from a monarchy to a republic. Understandably, it was also one of the most controversial events of the French Revolution.

Even before his death, Louis XVI's power had been dwindling steadily. Louis XVI and his family made a failed attempt to flee the country in June 1791, but the royal family was captured and returned to the castle, where they were placed under strict house arrest. That September Louis XVI, as a condition for resuming some of his royal powers, took an oath wherein he promised to obey the new constitution, which called for a hereditary constitutional monarchy, elected judges, and a single elected chamber (the Legislative Assembly) that would make all the laws. However, as Norah Lofts and Margery Weiner point out in *Eternal France: A History of France from the French Revolution Through World War II:* "[His] power was so diminished as to be virtually non-existent; Louis now held what authority he had from the nation, not by divine right, no longer King of France, but King of the French." Even under those adverse conditions, Louis XVI remained king for one more year. On September 21, 1792, the monarchy was abolished and the Legislative Assembly was replaced with a National Convention, a new government whose representatives would be elected through universal suffrage. The French Republic was born.

For the radical revolutionary leaders known as the Jacobins, however, stripping the king of his powers was not enough. On December 11, 1792, the Convention brought thirty-three articles of indictment against Louis XVI (now known as Louis Capet). The charges included the former king's decision to suspend the National Assembly on June 20, 1789, which suggested his unwillingness to move France toward representative government, and his attempt to escape France with a false passport. A trial against the erstwhile king led to Louis's conviction.

With Louis's guilt ascertained, the next issue was determining his fate. Not surprisingly, Jacobin leader Maximilien Robespierre was a strong voice in favor of the king's death. Robespierre argued that the French Revolution could not coexist with a king still living and asserted that Louis XVI must die in order to ensure the revolution's success. He explained, "Regretfully I speak this fatal truth: Louis must die because the nation must live. . . . A people that is still fighting for its freedom after so much sacrifice and so many battles; a people for whom the laws are not yet irrevocable except for the needy; a people for whom tyranny is still a crime subject to dispute: such a people should want to be avenged." Others were more lenient, including Anglo-American political philosopher Thomas Paine. Known for his political pamplets *Common Sense* and *The Rights of Man*, Paine had lived in France for several years and was a deputy in the assembly. He acknowledged that Louis XVI's regime had been marked by "intrigues, . . . falsehood, corruption, and rooted depravity." However, the political writer suggested that rather than sentence the king to death, the assembly should exile the former royal family to America, where Louis XVI could learn that "true system of government consists in fair, equal and honorable representation." Paine's suggestion and others that would have spared the king's life were rejected, and the sentence of death passed in the Convention by a vote of 361 to 288 on January 20, 1793. Louis was led to the guillotine the next day.

The death of the former king was undoubtedly one of the most contentious events of the French Revolution. However, other controversial events, such as the storming of the Bastille and the Reign of Terror, occurred during the revolutionary decade. The authors in the following chapter offer differing views on critical moments during the French Revolution.

Viewpoint 1

"I was continually subject to swords, bayonets, and pistols pressed against my body. . . . Already two of my soldiers had been assassinated behind me by the furious people."

Violence at the Bastille Was Caused by French Rioters

Louis de Flue

The Bastille was a large fortress and prison located on the outskirts of Paris. On July 14, 1789, a large crowd of French citizens—who doubted the sincerity of King Louis XVI's support for economic and financial reforms—stormed the Bastille in search of weapons in case the king ordered his troops to attack the city. The march on the fortress and its capture by the crowd resulted in the deaths of ninety-eight civilians and the execution of the Bastille's governor, Marquis de Launay, along with several other key officers. In the following viewpoint Louis de Flue, an officer stationed at the Bastille, describes his experiences defending the Bastille and criticizes the actions of the crowd. He supports the decisions made by de Launay, explaining that the governor ordered his troops not to fire upon the crowd. In ad-

Louis de Flue, "Rélation de la Prise de le Bastille le 14 Juillet 1789 par un de ses Defenseurs," *Révue Retrospective*, vol. 4. Paris: M.J. Taschereau, 1834.

dition, de Flue criticizes the violent and insulting behavior of the besiegers.

Having received orders from the Baron de Bezenval, I left on 7 July at 2 in the morning with a detachment of 32 men . . . we crossed Paris without difficulty and arrived at the Bastille where I entered with my troops. . . . During my next few days there, the Governor [Marquis de Launay] showed me around the place, the spots he thought the strongest and those the weakest. He showed me all the precautions that he had taken. . . . He complained of the small size of his garrison and of the impossibility of guarding the place if attacked. I told him his fears were unfounded, that the place was well fortified and that the garrison was sufficient if each would do his duty to defend it. . . .

Preparing for an Attack

The 12th of July we learned in the Bastille that there was the possibility of an attack on the gunpowder in the Arsenal. . . . Consequently, that night a detachment transported the powder to the Bastille where it was placed in the wells, poorly covered. That same night the goverer ordered the troops to remain inside the chateau, not wanting to have to defend the exterior in case of an attack.

During the day of the 13th, from the high towers of the Bastille, various fires were seen burning around the city, and we feared something similar near us, which would endanger the powder in the Bastille. . . . We learned the same day from some of the citizenry of the neighborhood that they were alarmed to see canons trained on the city and we learned at the same time that the National Guard was being mobilized to defend the city. Hearing this news, the Governor ordered . . . the fortress be sealed off.

. . . About three o'clock in the afternoon, a troop of armed citizens mixed with some soldiers came to attack from the Arsenal. They entered without difficulty into the courtyard. . . . They cut the chains holding the drawbridge, and it fell open; this operation was easily carried out because the Governor had ordered his troops not to fire before having warned them to leave, which we could not do while they were still at such a distance [from the fortress]. Nevertheless, the besiegers fired first on the high towers. . . .

After having easily dropped the bridge, they easily knocked down the door with axes and entered into the courtyard, where the governor went to meet them. He asked them what they wanted . . . and the general cry went up to "Lower the bridges!". . . The governor responded he could not and withdrew, ordering his troops to take up defensive positions. . . . The sieging forces brought their cannons to the gates. . . . I stationed my men to the left of the gate. . . .

I waited for the moment when the governor [was] to execute his threat and I was very surprised to see him send four veterans to the gates to open them and to lower the bridges. The crowd entered right away and disarmed us in an instant . . . in the castle, archives were thrown from the windows and everything was pillaged. The soldiers, including myself, who had left our packs in the castle had their personal effects taken. However, at that moment, this was not the mistreatment which worried us; we were menaced with being massacred in all manner possible. Finally, the furor . . . calmed a bit and I along with part of my troupe was conducted to the City Hall.

Encounter at the City Hall

During the trip, the streets and the houses, even the roofs, were full of crowds who insulted me and cursed me. I was continually subject to swords, bayonets, and pistols pressed against my body. I did not know how I was going to die but I was sure I was at my final moment. Those without arms threw stones at me, and women grimaced their teeth at me and menaced me with their fists. Already two of my soldiers had been assassinated behind me by the furious people. . . .

I arrived finally to general cries that I should be hung and at several hundred paces from the City Hall, when a head on a pike was brought before me to consider and I was told that it was Marquis de Launay [governor of the Bastille]. Crossing the place de Greve,[1]

---

1. An important political center during the revolution, the place de Greve was a Parisian meeting place and execution site.

The Bastille Was Not Inhumane

Conditions [at the Bastille] varied widely. The infamous subterranean *cachots*, slimy with damp and overrun with vermin, were no longer in use by the reign of Louis XVI, but the *calottes* immediately below the roof were almost as bad, since they took in snow and rain in the winter and almost asphyxiated prisoners with heat in the summer. For the majority of prisoners, however, conditions were by no means as bad as in other prisons, in particular the horrors that prevailed at Bicêtre. (For that matter, compared with what twentieth-century tyrannies have provided, the Bastille was paradise.) Sums were allotted to the governor for the subsistence of different ranks: fifteen livres a day for *conseillers* of the Parlement, nine for *bourgeois* and three for commoners. Paradoxically, "men of letters," who created the myth of a fortress of atrocities, were allotted the highest sum of nineteen livres a day. Even granting that the governor and his *service* undoubtedly made a profit on these allowances, they were considerably above the level at which most of the population of France attempted to subsist.

Simon Schama, *Citizens*, 1989.

I was passed before the body of Marquis de Lorme [guardian of City Hall] who was on the ground in a bath of his own blood. . . .

I was brought inside the City Hall and presented to a committee seated there. I was accused of being one of those who had put up resistance at the Bastille and that I was also the cause of blood being spilled. I justified myself better than I thought possible, saying that I had been under orders. . . . Not seeing any other means of saving myself and . . . what remained of my troops, I declared my willingness to serve the City and the Nation. . . . This appeared to them convincing; there was applause and a general cry of "bravo!" which I hoped would grant me a pardon. Instantly, I was brought wine and we had to drink to the health of the City and the Nation.

. . . We were taken to the Palais Royal and toured around the gardens to show to the people. . . . At that moment there arrived a prisoner freshly released from the Bastille, and we were taken equally for freed prisoners, so that the crowd showed great compassion for us. Some even claimed to be able to see the marks on our hands of the irons from which we had just been freed. Finally . . . an orator approached us and showed us to the people, to whom he spoke and explained that we had . . . been imprisoned by our officers . . . because we had refused to fire upon the citizens and that we deserved the esteem of the people . . . and a basket was passed around to take up a collection for us.

Renewed Opposition

[That night] I believed myself saved . . . and still in that belief, I was resting on a bench, having not slept for several nights [when I learned of the testimony of some of the soldiers at the Bastille] that I had ordered them to fire and that I had been the cause of the resistence . . . and that without me, they would have doubtlessly surrendered the place without firing. . . . This renewed the opposition to me such that . . . I was menaced and insulted again, and told that the affair was not yet over for me and my destiny would be settled the next day.

The next morning, Monsieur Ricart [secretary of the royal troops] procured for me a laisser-passer [a passport] and I was advised by Marquis de La Fayette to wear civilian clothing, which allowed me to go freely throughout Paris. . . .

As for the story that was told and which has been generally received that M. de Launay [the governor] had ordered the bridges lowerd to let in the crowd and that after, he had ordered them raised and ordered to fire on those who had entered [the courtyard], this story has no need to be refuted. Anyone who knows what a drawbridge is knows that having lowered one enough to let a crowd enter can no longer raise it again at will. Moreover, it is impossible that the garrison fired on those who had entered the courtyard because as soon as the crowd entered, we were all disarmed.

Viewpoint 2

"Veteran armies inured to War have never performed greater prodigies of valour than this leaderless multitude of persons belonging to every class."

Violence at the Bastille Was Caused by French Troops

Keversau

In the following viewpoint a French citizen named Keversau explains his role in the taking of the Bastille on July 14, 1789. A large crowd stormed the Bastille, the site of a large fortress and prison, in order to search for weapons to use against King Louis XVI, should he renege on proposed economic and political reforms and instruct his troops to attack Paris. More than one hundred people, including the governor of the Bastille, died in the attack. Keversau argues that the crowd behaved bravely despite being fired upon by the Bastille's soldiers and praises the freeing of seven prisoners.

V eteran armies inured to War have never performed greater prodigies of valour than this leaderless multitude of persons belonging to every class, workmen of all trades who, mostly ill-

Keversau, "A Conqueror of the Bastille Speaks," *The French Revolution*, edited by Georges Pernoud and Sabine Flaissier, translated by Richard Graves. New York: Capricorn Books, 1961.

equipped and unused to arms, boldly affronted the fire from the ramparts and seemed to mock the thunderbolts the enemy hurled at them. Their guns were equally well served. Cholat, the owner of a wine shop, who was in charge of a cannon installed in the garden of the Arsenal[1] was deservedly praised, as was Georges a gunner who arrived from Brest that same morning and was wounded in the thigh.

Overtaking the Fortress

The attackers having demolished the first drawbridge and brought their guns into position against the second could not fail to capture the fort. The Marquis de Launay (Governor of the Bastille) could doubtless have resisted the capture of the first bridge more vigorously, but this base agent of the despots, better fitted to be a gaoler, than the military commander of a fortress lost his head as soon as he saw himself hemmed in by the enraged people and hastened to take refuge behind his massive bastions. . . .

The people infuriated by the treachery of the Governor, who had fired on their representatives, took these offers of peace for another trap and continued to advance, firing as they went up to the drawbridge leading to the interior of the fort. A Swiss officer addressing the attackers through a sort of loop-hole near the drawbridge asked permission to leave the fort with the honours of war. "No, no," they cried. He then passed through the same opening a piece of paper, which those outside could not read because of the distance, calling out at the same time that he was willing to surrender, if they promised not to massacre his troops. . . .

The French Guards, who kept their heads in the hour of danger, formed a human barrier on the other side of the bridge to prevent the crowd of attackers from getting on to it. This prudent maneuver saved the lives of thousands of persons who would have fallen into the fosse.

About two minutes later one of the Invalides [resident of a home for old soldiers] opened the gate behind the drawbridge and asked what we wanted. "The surrender of the Bastille," was the answer, on which he let us in. . . .

---

1. The Arsenal was the area of the Bastille where weapons were stored.

A large crowd stormed the Bastille on July 14, 1789.

The Invalides were drawn up in line on the right and the Swiss on the left. They had stood their arms up against the wall. They clapped their hands and cried "bravo" to the besiegers, who came crowding into the fortress. Those who came in first treated the conquered enemy humanely and embraced the staff officers to show there was no ill-feeling. But a few soldiers posted on the platforms and unaware that the fortress had surrendered, discharged their muskets whereupon the people, transported with rage, threw themselves on the Invalides and used them with the utmost violence. One of them was massacred, the unfortunate Béquart, the brave soldier who had deserved so well of the town of Paris, when he stayed the hand of the Governor at the moment when he was on the point of blowing up the Bastille. Béquart, who had not fired a single shot throughout the day suffered two sword thrusts and had his hand cut off at the wrist by the stroke of a saber. Afterwards they carried in triumph round the streets this very hand to which so many citizens owed their safety. Béquart himself was dragged from the fortress and brought to la Grève.[2] The blind mob mistaking him for an artilleryman bound him to a gibbet where he died along with Asselin, the victim, like him, of a fatal mistake. All the officers were seized and their quarters were invaded by the mob, who smashed the furniture, the doors and the windows. In the general turmoil the people in the courtyard fired on those who were in the private quarters and on the platforms. Several were killed. The gallant Humbert received a musket ball as he stood on the platform and one of his comrades was killed in his arms. Then Arné, a brave fellow, fixed his grenadier's headdress on the point of his bayonet and showed himself over the top of the parapet, risking his life in order to stop the firing. . . .

Freeing the Prisoners

In the intoxication of victory the unfortunate inmates of the dungeons of the Bastille had been forgotten. All the keys had been carried off in triumph and it was necessary to force the doors of the cells. Seven prisoners were found and brought to the Palais Royal. These poor fellows were in transports of pleasure and could scarcely realize they were not the dupes of a dream, soon to be dispelled. But soon they perceived the dripping head of their tormentor stuck up on the point of a pike, above which was a placard bearing the words: "de Launay, Governor of the Bastille, disloyal and treacherous enemy of the people." At this sight tears of joy flowed from their eyes and they raised their hands to the skies to bless their first moments of liberty.

The keys were handed to Monsieur Brissot de Warville, who, a few years before, had been thrown into these caverns of despotism. Three thousand men were sent to guard these hated towers pending the issue of a decree ordering their destruction in accordance with the will of the people.

2. Paris's traditional spot for protests, located in front of City Hall

Viewpoint 3

"The French are the first people in the world who have established a true democracy."

The Founding of a French Republic Is an Important Achievement

Maximilien Robespierre

King Louis XVI's control over France, which had been increasingly limited since 1789, officially ended on August 10, 1792, when the Legislative Assembly voted to suspend the king from his duties. That decision led to the creation of the French Republic on September 22, 1792. In the following viewpoint Maximilien Robespierre, in an address to France's legislature, argues that the republic is vital to the French people because only republics and democracies can provide peace and happiness to their citizens. According to Robespierre, France is the first true democracy because it has made all male citizens equal under the laws. He concludes that the republic will prosper if the French people and their representatives remain virtuous and subordinate their private desires to the public good. Robespierre was a leader of the Jacobin faction, a radical political party that led

Maximilien Robespierre, address before the legislature of France, February 5, 1794.

France until July 1794, when Robespierre and other important Jacobin figures were arrested and executed.

We wish, to fulfill the intentions of nature and the destiny of humanity, realize the promises of philosophy, and acquit providence of the long reign of crime and tyranny. We wish that France, once illustrious among enslaved nations, may, while eclipsing the glory of all the free peoples that ever existed, become a model to nations, a terror to oppressors, a consolation to the oppressed, an ornament of the universe; and that, by sealing our work with our blood, we may witness at least the dawn of universal happiness—this is our ambition, this is our aim.

What kind of government can realize these prodigies? A democratic or republican government only; these two terms are synonymous notwithstanding the abuse of common language; for aristocracy is no more the republic than is monarchy. A democracy is not a state where the people, always assembled, regulate by themselves all public affairs, and still less one where one hundred thousand portions of the people, by measures that are isolated, hasty, and contradictory, would decide the fate of the whole society: such a government has never existed and could not exist except to return the people to despotism.

A democracy is a state where the sovereign people, guided by laws of their own making, do for themselves everything that they can do well, and by means of delegates everything that they cannot do for themselves.

The Principles of Democracy

It is therefore in the principles of democratic government that you must seek the rules of your political conduct.

But in order to found democracy and consolidate it among us, in order to attain the peaceful reign of constitutional laws, we must complete the war of liberty against tyranny and weather successfully the tempests of the revolution; such is the aim of the revolutionary government that you have organized. You must therefore still regulate your conduct by the stormy circumstances in which the republic finds itself, and the plan of your administration should be the result of the spirit of the revolutionary government combined with the general principles of democracy.

And what is the fundamental principle of a democratic or popular government; in other words, what is the mainspring which supports it and gives it motion? It is virtue; I speak of the public virtue which produced so many prodigies in Greece and Rome, and which should produce still more wonderful prodigies in republican France; of that virtue which is nothing else than love of the *patrie* [fatherhood] and its laws.

But as the essence of the republic or of democracy is equality, it follows that love of one's country necessarily includes love of equality.

Again, it is true that this sublime passion supposes a preference for the public interest over all private considerations; whence it results that love of country still supposes or produces all the virtues; for what are they but a strength of soul which makes possible such sacrifices, and how could the slave of avarice or ambition, for example, sacrifice his idol to his country's welfare?

Virtue and Equality

Not only is virtue the soul of democracy, but it can exist in no other government. In a monarchy, I know of only one individual who can love his country, and who for this does not even need virtue; it is the monarch. The reason is that of all the inhabitants of his dominions the monarch alone has a *patrie*. Is he not sovereign at least in practice? Does he not assume the prerogative of the people? And what is the *patrie* if it is not the country where one is a citizen and a member of the sovereign?

By a natural consequence of this principle, in aristocratic states the word *patrie* means nothing for any but the patrician families who have usurped the sovereignty.

It is only in democracies that the state is truly the *patrie* of all the individuals who compose it, and can count as many defenders of its cause as there are citizens. This is the source of the superiority of free people over all others. If Athens and Sparta triumphed over the tyrants of Asia, and the Swiss over the tyrants of Spain and Austria, no other cause need be sought.

But the French are the first people in the world who have established true democracy by calling all men to equality and to full enjoyment of the rights of citizenship; and that is, in my opinion, the true reason why all the tyrants leagued against the republic will be vanquished.

There are from this moment great conclusions to be drawn from the principles that we have just laid down.

Proper Political Conduct

Since virtue and equality are the soul of the republic, and your aim is to found and to consolidate the republic, it follows that the first rule of your political conduct must be to relate all of your measures to the maintenance of equality and to the development of virtue; for the first care of the legislator must be to strengthen the principles on which the government rests. Hence all that tends to excite a love of country, to purify moral standards, to exalt souls, to direct the passions of the human heart toward the public good must be adopted or established by you. All that tends to concentrate and debase them into selfish egotism, to awaken an infatuation for trivial things, and scorn for great ones, must be rejected or repressed by you. In the system of the French revolution, that which is immoral is impolitic, and that which tends to corrupt is counterrevolutionary. Weakness, vices, and prejudices are the road to monarchy. Carried away, too often perhaps, by the force of ancient habits, as well as by the tendency of human nature to be attracted by false ideas and pusillanimous sentiments, we have much less need to defend ourselves from excesses of energy than from excesses of weakness. The most dangerous shoal that we have to avoid is not perhaps warmth of zeal but rather that lassitude which ease produces and a distrust of our own courage. Therefore tighten continually the spring of republican government, instead of letting it run down. I need not say that I am not here justifying any excess. The most sacred principles may be abused; the wisdom of government should take account of circumstances, time its measures, choose its means; for the manner of preparing for great accomplishments is an essential part of the talent for producing them, just as wisdom is itself an attribute of virtue.

We do not claim to model the French Republic after that of

Sparta; we wish to give it neither the austere manners nor the corruption of a cloister. We have just presented to you the essence of the moral and political principle of a popular government. You have, therefore, a compass to direct you through the tempest of the passions and the whirlwind of the intrigues that surround you. You have the touchstone with which you can test all your laws, all the propositions that are laid before you. By comparing them always with this principle, you may henceforth avoid the rock on which large assemblies usually split, the danger of being taken by surprise, and of hasty, incoherent, and contradictory measures. You can give to all your actions the systematic unity, the wisdom, and the dignity that should characterize the representatives of the first people of the world.

There is no need to detail the obvious consequences of the principle of democracy; it is the principle itself, simple yet fruitful, which deserves to be developed.

Republican virtue may be considered in relation to the people and in relation to the government: it is necessary in both. When the government alone lacks it, there remains the resource of the people's virtue; but when the people themselves are corrupted, liberty is already lost.

Guarding Against Corruption

Fortunately virtue is natural in the people, aristocratic prejudices notwithstanding. A nation is truly corrupt when, after having, by degrees, lost its character and liberty, it passes from democracy to aristocracy or monarchy; this is the death of the political body by decrepitude. When, after four hundred years of glory, avarice at length drove from Sparta the moral standards and laws of Lycurgus, Agis died in vain to restore them; Demosthenes in vain thundered against Philip; Philip found in the vices of degenerated Athens advocates more eloquent than Demosthenes. There is still as great a population in Athens as in the time of Miltiades and Aristides,[1] but there are no more Athenians. What does it matter that

---

1. Lycurgus established the Spartan constitution; Agis was a king of Sparta; Demosthenes was a Greek political orator; Philip was the ruler of Macedonia; Miltiades and Aristides were Athenian generals who helped lead the troops at Marathon.

Brutus has killed the tyrant [Julius Caesar]? Tyranny still lives in people's hearts, and Rome survives only in the person of Brutus.

But when, by prodigious efforts of courage and reason, a people breaks the chains of despotism to make trophies to liberty out of the pieces; when, by the force of moral vigor, they rise, in some manner from the arms of death, to resume all the strength of youth; when, by turns sensitive and proud, intrepid and docile, they can be checked neither by impregnable ramparts nor by innumerable armies of tyrants leagued against them, and yet of themselves they stop before the image of the law; if they do not rise rapidly to the height of their destiny, it can only be the fault of those who govern them.

Besides, there is a sense in which it may be said that to love justice and equality the people need no great virtue; it is sufficient that they love themselves.

But the magistrate is obliged to sacrifice his interest to that of the people, and the pride of office to equality. The law must speak with special authority to those who are its organs. The power of the government must be felt by its own agents to keep all its parts in harmony with the law. If there is a representative body, a primary authority constituted by the people, it is the duty of that body to superintend and repress continually all public functionaries. But what will keep *it* within proper bounds other than its own virtue? The more exalted this source of public order is, the purer it must be; the representative body must therefore begin by subjecting all its own private passions to a general passion for the public good. Happy the representatives when their glory and their own interests attach them as much as their duty to the cause of liberty.

Let us deduce from all this an important truth: that the character of a popular government is to place its confidence in the people and be severe toward itself.

Viewpoint 4

"A large republic is impossible, since there has never been a large republic."

The French Republic Will Not Last

Joseph de Maistre

In the following viewpoint Joseph de Maistre argues that the French Republic, which was established on September 22, 1792, following the abolition of the monarchy, cannot succeed. According to de Maistre, a large republic in which all people are represented cannot exist because in the course of history one has never been established; he contends that the republic recently created in America (the United States) has yet to prove its longevity. In addition, de Maistre asserts that the French republic will fail because a durable government cannot be built upon a corrupt and savage revolution. De Maistre was a French writer, diplomat, and royalist whose works include *Considerations on France*, the source of the following selection.

W hat could have been said to the French to get them to believe in a republic of twenty-four million people? Two things only: (1) nothing prevents us from doing something that has never been seen before; (2) the discovery of the representative system makes possible for us what was impossible for our prede-

Joseph de Maistre, *Considerations on France*, 1797.

cessors. Let us examine the strength of these two arguments.

If we are told that a die thrown a billion times had never turned up anything but five numbers—1, 2, 3, 4, and 5—could we believe that there was a 6 on one of the faces? NO, undoubtedly; and it would be as obvious to us as if we had seen it that one of the faces is blank or that one of the numbers is repeated.

Well then! Let us run through history; there you will see so-called *Fortune* tirelessly throwing the die for over four thousand years. Has LARGE REPUBLIC ever been rolled? No. Therefore, that *number* is not on the die.

If the world had seen the successive development of new forms of government, we would have no right to affirm that such-and-such a form of government is impossible because it has never been seen. But things are exactly the opposite; monarchies have always existed, and sometimes republics. If we want to go into the subdivisions, we can call government where the masses exercise sovereignty *democracy*, and that where sovereignty belongs to a more or less restricted number of privileged families *aristocracy*. And everything has been said.

The comparison with the die is perfectly exact; the same numbers always coming from the horn of Fortune, we are authorized by the theory of probabilities to affirm that there are no others.

Large Republics Cannot Exist

Let us not confuse the essences of things with their modifications: the first are unalterable and always remain the same, the second change and vary the spectacle a little, at least for the multitude; but every experienced eye will easily penetrate the changing cloak with which eternal nature is enveloped according to time and place.

For example, what is peculiar and new about the three powers that constitute the government of England? The names of the *Peers* and the *Commons*, the costumes of the lords, etc. But the three powers, considered in the abstract, are to be found wherever a wise and lasting liberty is to be found; above all, they were found in Sparta, where the government, before Lycurgus,[1] 'was always in oscillation, inclining at one time to tyranny when the kings had

---

1. Lycurgus wrote the Spartan constitution in the seventh century B.C.

too much power and at another time to popular confusion when the common people had usurped too much authority'. But Lycurgus placed the senate between the two, so that it was, according to Plato, 'a salutary counterweight . . . and a strong barrier holding the two extremities in equal balance and giving a firm and assured foundation to the health of the state, because the senators . . . ranged themselves on the side of the king when there was need to resist popular temerity, and on the other hand, just as strongly took the part of the people against the king to prevent the latter from usurping a tyrannical power'.

Thus, nothing is new, and a large republic is impossible, since there has never been a large republic.

The History of Representative Government

As for the representative system, which some people believe capable of resolving the problem, I hope I will be pardoned for a digression.

Let us begin by noting that this system is by no means a modern discovery, but was a *production*, or better, a *piece*, of feudal government when the latter attained that state of maturity and equilibrium which made it, all things considered, the most perfect in the world.

Having formed the communes, the royal authority called them to the national assemblies; they could appear there only through their mandatories, and this is how the representative system began.

In passing, the same thing may be said of trial by jury. Within the hierarchy of tenures the vassals of the same order were called to the courts of their respective suzerains; from this was born the maxim that every man must be judged by his peers (*Pares curtis*). The English have maintained the idea in its full extent and have even developed it from its original sense; but the French, less tenacious, or ceding perhaps to invincible circumstances, have not extended it to the same degree.

One would have to be incapable of penetrating to what [Francis] Bacon calls the *interiora rerum* [inside of things] to imagine that men could have erected such institutions by anterior reasoning or that they could be the fruit of deliberation.

Moreover, national representation is not peculiar to England: it is to be found in every European monarchy; although it is alive in Great Britain, elsewhere it is dead or sleeping. To consider if its suspension is humanity's misfortune or if we should return to the old forms is beyond the scope of this little work. Let the following historical observations suffice: (1) in England, where national representation has gained and retained more strength than anywhere else, there is no mention of such a thing before the thirteenth century; (2) the system was not an invention, or the result of deliberation, or the result of the action of the people making use of their ancient rights, but was, in reality, the work of an ambitious soldier, who, after the battle of Lewes,[2] created the balance of the three powers without knowing what he was *doing*, as always happens; (3) not only was the convocation of the Commons to the National Council a concession of the monarch, but in the beginning the king named the representatives of the provinces, cities, and boroughs; (4) even after the Commons arrogated to themselves the right of sending representatives to Parliament during Edward I's journey to Palestine [or the Ninth Crusade], they had there only a consultative voice; they presented their *grievances*, like the Estates-General[3] in France, and the formula for the concessions emanating from the throne as a result of their petitions was always *Granted by the King and the spiritual and temporal lords on the humble prayers of the Commons;* and finally (5) the attribution of co-legislative power to the House of Commons is still quite new, since it scarcely goes back to the middle of the fifteenth century.

So if the phrase 'national representation' is understood to mean a *certain* number of representatives sent by *certain* men taken from *certain* cities and boroughs by virtue of an old concession by the sovereign, there is no dispute—such a government exists, and it is that of England. But if the phrase is understood to mean that *all* the people are represented, that they may be represented only by virtue of a mandate, and that every citizen, with some physically and morally inevitable exceptions, is able to give or receive these mandates, and if there is also a claim to join to such an order of things the abolition of all hereditary distinctions and of-

2. The battle of Lewes (1264) was a victory for the barons, led by Simon de Montfort, over King Henry III.   3. A legislative body that met originally prior to 1789.

fices, this representation is a thing that has never been seen and that will never succeed.

America is often cited. I know of nothing so provoking as the praises bestowed on this babe-in-arms. Let it grow.

Evaluating the French Proposal

But to make this discussion as clear as possible, we must note that the instigators of the French Republic are bound to prove not only that *perfected* representation (so styled by the innovators) is possible and good, but also that the people can by this means retain their sovereignty (again, so they say) and form, in their totality, a republic. This is the crux of the question, for if the *republic* is in the capital and the rest of France is *subject* to the republic, the republic is not accountable to the *sovereign people.*

The . . . commission that was charged with proposing a method of national representation estimated the French population at thirty million. Let us accept this number and assume that France keeps her conquests. Each year, according to the terms of the constitution, two hundred and fifty members of the legislative body will be replaced by two hundred and fifty others. So if the assumed fifteen million males in the population were immortal, qualified as representatives, and named in rotation, then each Frenchman would exercise his turn at national sovereignty once in every sixteen thousand years. But since some men cannot be prevented from dying from time to time in this interval, and since moreover, some people may be elected more than once, and since many individuals, by nature and good sense, will always be ineligible as national representatives, the imagination is staggered by the prodigious number of sovereigns condemned to die without having reigned.

[Jean-Jacques] Rousseau maintained that *the national will cannot be delegated;* one may agree or not and debate such academic questions a thousand years, but what is sure is that the representative system directly excludes the exercise of sovereignty, especially in the French system, where the rights of the people are limited to selecting electors and where not only are the people unable to give special mandates to their representatives, but the law carefully severs all relations between representatives and their respective provinces by warning them that *they are not sent by those who sent them*, but by the *nation*, a wonderfully convenient word, since one makes of it whatever one wishes. In short, it is impossible to imagine a system better calculated to annihilate the rights of the people.

Thus that vile Jacobin conspirator [François-Noël Babeuf] was quite right when he declared roundly during a judicial inquiry, 'I believe the present government a usurper of authority, a violator of all the rights of the people, who have been reduced to the most deplorable slavery. It is a frightful system of the happiness of the few founded on the oppression of the masses. The people are so muzzled, so loaded with chains by this aristocratic government, that it is becoming more difficult than ever for them to break them.'

So what does this vain honour of representation mean to the *nation* when it is involved so indirectly and when millions of individuals will never participate? Are sovereignty and government any less alien to them?

Liberty Is Not the Issue

But, they say in answering the argument, what does it matter to the nation whether representation is a vain honour, if the system establishes public liberty?

This is not the question. The question is not whether the French people can be *free* with the constitution they have been given, but whether they can be *sovereign*. They change the question to escape the logic. Let us begin by excluding the exercise of sovereignty and insist on the fundamental point that the sovereign will always be in Paris, that all this noise about representation means nothing, that the *people* remain perfectly alien to government, that they are more subject than they were under a monarchy, and that the phrase *large republic*, like *square circle*, is self-contradictory. Moreover, the argument has been demonstrated arithmetically.

The question may be reduced to finding out whether the interests of the French people are served by being *subject* to an executive directory and two councils as instituted by the 1795 constitution rather than to a king reigning according to the old forms. There is much less difficulty in resolving a problem than in posing it.

So we must discard this word *republic* and speak only of the government. I will not discuss whether or not this government is fit to secure the public welfare; the French know the answer well enough! But given its nature, no matter what it is called, let us see if one may believe in its permanence.

Let us first of all raise ourselves to a level that befits an intelligent being, and from this elevated point of view, consider the origins of this government.

Evil has nothing in common with life; it cannot create, since its power is purely negative. *Evil is the schism of being; it is not true.*

A Uniquely Bad Event

Now what distinguishes the French Revolution and makes it an *event* unique in history is that it is radically *bad.* No element of good disturbs the eye of the observer; it is the highest degree of corruption ever known; it is pure impurity.

On what page of history will you find such a great quantity of vices assembled at one time on the same stage? What a horrible assemblage of baseness and cruelty! What profound immorality! What absence of all decency!

The characteristics of the springtime of liberty are so striking that it is impossible to be mistaken. It is a time when love of the fatherland is a religion and respect for the laws a superstition, a time of sturdy character and austere morals, when every virtue flourishes at the same time, when factions benefit the fatherland because they fight only for the honour of serving it, when everything, even crime, carries the mark of greatness.

If this picture is compared to the one offered us by France, how can anyone believe in the permanence of a liberty that springs from gangrene? Or, more precisely, how can one believe that this liberty can be born (since it does not as yet exist) or that from the heart of the most disgusting corruption there can emerge the form of government that less than any other may dispense with virtue? When one hears these so-called republicans talk of liberty and virtue, one thinks of a faded courtesan with rouged blushes putting on the airs of a virgin.

A republican journal reports the following anecdote on Parisian morals today: 'A case of seduction was pleaded before the Civil Tribunal. A young girl of fourteen astonished the judges by a degree of corruption that more than matched the profound immorality of her seducer. More than half the audience was composed of young women and young girls; among them more than twenty were no more than thirteen or fourteen, several being with their mothers. And instead of covering their faces, they laughed loudly at the necessary but disgusting details that made the men blush.'

I ask the reader to recall that Roman citizen who, in the days of Roman greatness, was punished for having embraced his wife before his children. Draw the parallel and your own conclusion.

No doubt the French Revolution has lasted long enough to go through several phases; nevertheless, its general character has never varied, and from its birth there was evidence of what it would become. There was a certain inexplicable delirium, a blind impetuosity, a scandalous contempt for everything respectable, a new kind of atrocity that joked about its crimes, and especially, an impudent prostitution of reasoning and of every word meant to express ideas of justice and virtue. . . .

So can a durable government emerge from this bloody mire? To be sure the savage and licentious morals of barbarian peoples have not prevented their eventual civilization; barbarous ignorance has no doubt presided over the establishment of a number of political systems, but learned barbarism, systematic atrocity, calculated corruption, and, above all, irreligion have never produced anything. Greenness leads to maturity; rottenness leads to nothing.

Viewpoint 5

"In 1793 terrorist discourse was in the mouths of nearly all the leaders of the Revolution."

The Reign of Terror Was Caused by Jacobin Leadership

François Furet

The rule of Maximilien Robespierre and other members of the radical Jacobin party is best remembered for the Terror, when more than thirty thousand people were executed in France between 1793 and 1794. In the following viewpoint François Furet criticizes the Terror and disputes the arguments made by scholars wishing to defend the revolutionaries. Furet asserts that the Terror was not necessary to ensure public safety but was conducted to silence counterrevolutionaries and others who threatened Jacobin rule. He also argues that the Terror exacerbated the civil war that beset France in 1783. Furet was a professor at the University of Chicago and a leading scholar of the French Revolution whose works include *Interpreting the French Revolution* and *A Critical Dictionary of the French Revolution*.

The legacy of the Terror poisoned all subsequent revolutionary history and, beyond that, all political life in nineteenth-century

François Furet, *A Critical Dictionary of the French Revolution*, edited by François Furet and Mona Ozouf, translated by Arthur Goldhammer. Cambridge, MA: Harvard University Press, 1981. Copyright © 1981 by the President and Fellows of Harvard College. Reproduced by permission.

France. Throughout the Thermidorian period[1] the Terror lurked about the fringes of the political scene. The royalists used it to forge a weapon of revenge, an instrument for settling local scores in areas where the population leaned toward their camp and Republican troops were thinly scattered, as in the Rhône valley. The republicans would have liked to forget the Terror and root the new institutions of the Year III [September 1794 to September 1795] in the law; Benjamin Constant and Madame de Staël worked feverishly between 9 Thermidor and 18 Brumaire[2] to exorcise the ghost of the guillotine that haunted the Republic, but to no avail. Thermidor revived the royalist menace and counterrevolutionary violence, and the Directory[3] was unable to adhere to the legal election dates stipulated by the Constitution. In September 1797 [Pierre] Augereau's army laid siege to Paris at the behest of the director [Paul] Barras in order to save the Republic from a royalist parliamentary majority. The coup d'état of 18 Fructidor (September 5) was the signal for a new series of 'public safety' measures in which deportation to Guiana replaced the scaffold, with refractory priests paying the heavy price. The nation's revolutionary education proceeded on course, and the civil and military putsch of 18–19 Brumaire (9–10 November 1799) capped it off by establishing a regime 'that completed the Terror by replacing permanent revolution with permanent war' (Marx, *The Holy Family*).

In the nineteenth century memories of the Terror imparted a peculiar bitterness to civil struggle, while at the same time adding further passion to the great conflict between Ancien Régime[4] and Revolution. By associating the advent of democracy with a bloody

1. The Thermidorian period began in July 1794, following the arrests and overthrow of key Jacobin leaders. The Thermidorians were more moderate than Robespierre and his compatriots.   2. Benjamin Constant was a French-Swiss novelist and political writer who had a lengthy affair and eventually went into exile with fellow writer Madame de Staël. Born Anne Louise Germaine Necker, she was the daughter of Jacques Necker, a key figure in Louis XVI's government and a supporter of progressive politics. 9 Thermidor is July 27, 1794, when the major Jacobin leaders were arrested; on 18 Brumaire, or November 9, 1799, a coup d'etat made Napoleon Bonaparte the First Consul (and putative dictator) of France.   3. The Directory was a five-man executive board established in August 1795.   4. The Ancien Régime was the government prior to the French Revolution; the time of absolute monarchy.

dictatorship, it supplied counterrevolutionaries with arguments and liberals with fears. It embarrassed or divided republicans and isolated socialists. In postrevolutionary France the monarchy was suspect because of the Ancien Régime, but the Republic was unable to cleanse its image of the blood spilled in its name. When it finally triumphed in the 1870s, it was because the republicans had conquered their own demons and presented a pacified version of their great ancestors from which the spectre of the guillotine had been exorcised. It was not until the twentieth century, with the injection of bolshevism and the development of a communist extreme left, that a cult of the Terror, associated with that of [Maximilien] Robespierre, was established on grounds of revolutionary necessity, where for half a century it flourished in the shadow of the Soviet example.

Interpreting the Terror

Thus, there exists a history of the history of the Terror associated with the vicissitudes of French political history over the past two hundred years. But that history can also be written in a less chronological mode by attempting to reconstitute the various types of interpretation to which the Terror has been subjected.

The most common strategy is to relate the Terror to circumstances external to the Revolution; we are told, then, that the Terror was merely the product of the tragic situation in which the Republic found itself in 1793 and was a terrible yet necessary instrument of public safety. Surrounded by enemies foreign and domestic, the Convention [a legislature] allegedly had no choice but to rely on fear of the guillotine to mobilize men and resources. We find this interpretation being advanced by the Thermidorians in the period immediately following Robespierre's fall, and it was destined to enjoy a brilliant future, for it can also be found in most French public school texts for reasons that are easy to understand: it has the advantage of offering to the ultimately victorious republican tradition a revolution exonerated of guilt for the terrorist episode, responsibility for which is shifted to its adversaries. That is why this interpretation is favoured by many who consider themselves heirs of 1789, for it is a way of escaping the dilemma of contradiction or denial.

The 'circumstantial' thesis is often associated with another idea, according to which the Terror coincides with a period during which social strata other than the cultivated bourgeoisie were gaining access to power: specifically, the class of urban artisans and tradesmen from which the sans-culotte activists[5] were recruited and which [François] Mignet, for example, setting the tone for liberal historiography, dubbed the 'plebs' or the 'multitude' to distinguish them from the bourgeoisie of 1789. Thus circumstances presumably brought to the fore a second revolution, which lacks the historical dignity of the first because it was neither bourgeois nor liberal; its necessity was merely circumstantial, that is, subordinate to the principal course of the event, which continued to be defined by the principle of 1789 and the rise of the bourgeoisie. But the plebeian nature of this episode makes it political reflexes, at once egalitarian and punitive, triggered by military reverses and internal insurrections. The Ancien Régime had not known how to educate its people, and for this it paid a heavy price at the moment of its downfall.

It is not difficult to find elements of historical reality to support interpretations of this type. The Terror did in fact develop in the course of the Revolution at a time of foreign and domestic danger and out of obsession with 'aristocratic' treason and an 'aristocratic plot'. It continually justified itself in these terms as indispensable to the salvation of the fatherland. It was 'placed on the order of the day' and exercised in the name of the state and the Republic only under pressure from sans-culotte militants. The Paris prison massacres of September 1792 showed the extremes to which the punitive passions of the people might go. A year later, it was in part to channel those passions that the Convention and the Committees turned the Terror into a banner of government.

Nevertheless, neither the circumstances nor the political attitudes of the *petit peuple* [little people] are enough to account for the phenomenon. The 'circumstances', too, have a chronology. The risks for the Revolution were greatest at the beginning and in the middle of the summer of 1793, at a time when the activity of the Revo-

5. Sans-culottes were politically radical workers who were known for wearing long trousers in opposition to the breeches worn by aristocrats.

lutionary Tribunal was relatively minimal. By contrast, the Terror intensified with the improvement of the situation and the victories, starting in October. It reached a peak during the winter, in a Lyons that had been vanquished for several months and in a defeated Vendée that had to be put to the torch, as well as in countless other places where there were violent clashes as a result of initiatives on the part of local militants or envoys of the Convention. There was indeed a connection between the civil war and the Terror, but it was not that the Terror was an instrument for ending a war; it followed and actually prolonged rather than shortened the war. One cannot credit it with patriotic devotion without falling into inconsistency, because to do so would be to assume—incorrectly, by the way— the existence of a counter-revolutionary France. Nor can one credit it with saving the fatherland or maintaining the Republic, since it came after the victory 'The Great Terror', wrote the republican [Edgar] Quinet as long ago as 1867, 'nearly everywhere revealed itself after the victories. Can we maintain that it caused them? Can we argue that, in our systems, effect precedes cause?'

The explanation involving the role of popular attitudes accounts for only some of the facts. It is indeed true, as we have seen, that the pressure to establish a terrorist dictatorship came chiefly from sans-culotte militants. But it is not a simple matter to establish a dividing line between the 'people' and the political elites, between 'popular' culture and 'high' culture. What about [Jean-Paul] Marat, for example, who may be considered one of the purest ideologues of the Terror? To which group did he belong? This demi-savant, who since 1789 had been denouncing the aristocratic plot and tirelessly calling for scaffolds to be erected, straddled both 'cultures'. The same can be said of [Jacques-René] Hébert and the Hébertists, who extended his influence in Paris and played so important a role in the republican repression in Vendée.[6] In fact, in 1793 terrorist discourse was in the mouths of nearly all the leaders of the Revolution, including those who had no special relation to sans-culotte activism, the legists and bourgeois of the committees and the Convention. [Bertrand] Barère's demand in the sum-

---

6. Vendée was an area in western France that was the site of a counterrevolutionary movement.

mer of 1793 for the total destruction of the Vendée is enough to make clear the grip of terrorist fanaticism on all the Montagnard deputies.

Of course this call for widespread extermination grew out of the civil war, even if that was not its only cause. But, as Mona Ozouf has demonstrated, from the autumn of 1793 to the spring of 1794 the case for the necessity of the Terror abandoned the circumstantial grounds of the war in favor of a more fundamental justification: nothing less than the Revolution itself. After the end of March and the liquidation of the Hébertists, which put an end to the bloody escalation of what remained of sans-culottism, the Terror, by this point the exclusive instrument of the Robespierrist clan, had ceased to be a matter for learned and sometimes philosophical rationalization. It was less a part of the arsenal of victory than of an ambition for regeneration.

Nor was the climate any longer that of a besieged city, since the frontiers had been liberated and the civil war extinguished. The most obvious use of the guillotine was no longer the extermination of avowed enemies but rather that of 'factions': the Hébertists followed by the Dantonists [supporters of the Jacobin Georges-Jacques Danton]. The Terror raged all the more fiercely because the Robespierrist group had no further support either on its left, among the activists, or on its right, in public opinion; it was a government of fear, which Robespierre portrayed in theory as a government of virtue. Conceived in order to exterminate aristocracy, the Terror ended as a means of subduing wrongdoers and combatting crime. From now on it coincided with and was inseparable from the Revolution, because there was no other way of someday moulding a republic of citizens.

Hence the Terror cannot be reduced to circumstances, whether the emergency situation or pressure from the *petit peuple*, surrounding its birth. Not that circumstances played no role; obviously they provided an environment in which ideology developed and allowed terrorist institutions to be gradually put in place. But this ideology, present in the Revolution of 1789, predated the circumstances and enjoyed an independent existence, which was associated with the nature of French revolutionary culture through several sets of ideas.

Revolutionary Ideas

The first of these ideas was of man's regeneration, in which respect the Revolution was akin to a religious annunciation but in a secularized mode. The actors in the events actually conceived of their own history as an emancipation of man in general. The issue was not to reform French society but to reinstitute the social pact on the basis of man's free will; France represented only the first act of this decisive development. This truly philosophical ambition was unusual, however, in that it was constantly caught up in the test of actual history, as though the truth of a religious promise had been left to empirical verification by the facts. In the gap between facts and promise was born the idea of a regeneration, to reduce the distance between the Revolution and its ambition, which it could not renounce without ceasing to be itself. If the Republic of free citizens was not yet possible, it was because men, perverted by their past history, were wicked; by means of the Terror, the Revolution—a history without precedent, entirely new— would make a new man.

Another idea said roughly the same thing, or arrived at the same result: that politics could do anything. The revolutionary universe was a universe populated by wills, entirely animated by the conflict between good intentions and evil plans; no action was ever uncertain, no power ever innocent. As first [Georg] Hegel and later Marx recognized, the French Revolution was the theatre in which the voluntarism of modern politics revealed itself in all its purity. The event remained ever faithful to its original idea, according to which the social contract could be instituted only by free wills. This attribution of unlimited powers to political action opened a vast field to radicalization of conflicts and to militant fanaticism. Henceforth each individual could arrogate to himself what had once been a divine monopoly, that of creating the human world, with the ambition of recreating it. If he then found obstacles standing in his way, he attributed them to the perversity of adverse wills rather than to the opacity of things: the Terror's sole purpose was to do away with those adversaries.

In the end, the Revolution put the people in the place of the king. In order to restore to the social order the truth and justice ignored by the Ancien Régime, it returned the people to its rightful place, usurped for so long by the king: the place of sovereign. What the Revolution, following [philosopher Jean-Jacques] Rousseau, called the general will was radically different from monarchical power in the manner of its formation yet identical to it in the extent of its jurisdiction. The absolute sovereignty of the king presaged the sovereignty of democracy. Wholly obsessed with legitimacy, having thrown off divine guidance without establishing reciprocal checks and balances in the American manner, the Revolution was unwilling to set limits to public authority. It had lived since 1789 on the idea of a new absolute—and indivisible—sovereignty, which excluded pluralism of representation because it assumed the unity of the nation. Since that unity did not exist—and Girondin [a moderate political faction] federalism showed that factions continued to plot in the shadows—the function of the Terror, as well as of purging elections, was [invariably to] establish it.

Viewpoint 6

"The institutions of the Terror had been created long before [Maximilien] Robespierre joined the government on 26 July 1793."

The Reign of Terror Was Not Caused by Jacobin Leadership

Gwynne Lewis

The radical Jacobin government has often been blamed for the eventual failure of the French Revolution to form a lasting republic, in large part because of the thousands of executions (known collectively as the Terror) that occurred between 1793 and 1794 under the leadership of Jacobins such as Maximilien Robespierre and Georges-Jacques Danton. In the following viewpoint Gwynne Lewis defends the actions of these men and other Jacobin leaders. She argues that the moderate Girondin government that led France in 1792 and 1793, when the nation was at war, set the stage for the Terror by establishing the Revolutionary Tribunal (a court that held trials for accused political offenders) and the Committee of Public Safety (the chief executive body). Lewis also contends that most of the Jacobin leadership was uncomfortable with the more extreme politics advocated by groups such as the *enragés*, a small group of Parisian radical extremists who campaigned for strict economic controls. Lewis is a professor of history at the University of Warwick in Coventry, England, and the author of *The French Revolution: Rethinking the Debate*, the source of the following viewpoint.

From the summer of 1793 to the summer of 1794, the period known to history as 'The Terror', the Revolution was saved from its internal and external enemies, at considerable cost to human life and the infant political democracy of the early 1790s, symbolised by the famous Constitution of 1793. Published on 24 June, it was not only founded upon universal male suffrage but included the right to public assistance and to education, as well as the 'right to insurrection'. It was, of course, never implemented, since, formalised by the decree of 10 October 1793, the government of France was declared to be 'revolutionary until peace'. The fact that the Constitution of 1793 was stillborn underlines the immense gap—central to an understanding of the Revolution—which separated the political idealism of 1789 from the harsh socio-economic and military facts of life in that summer of 1793 when Jacobins and sansculottes[1] began to dominate the political scene in most towns and villages of France, a sword in one hand, a social policy in the other. The great political paradox of the Year II would be that whilst the Jacobins, desperate to unleash the energies of the nation for war, sought to satisfy the social and economic aspirations of the urban and rural masses, they were also creating the structures of a powerful State bureaucracy, civil and military, which would eventually be used to eject the mass of the public from a participatory democracy.

Jacobins Versus Girondins

Not that the Terror of 1793–4 should be identified too hurriedly with the Jacobins: the institutions of the Terror had been created

1. Translated as "without breeches," sansculottes were politically radical workers known for wearing long trousers, in opposition to the breeches worn by aristocrats. Jacobins were the radical leaders during the early years of the revolution.

long before [Maximilien] Robespierre joined the government on 26 July 1793. Following the downfall of the monarchy, France had been governed by a Council of Ministers supported by committees of the Convention, not the ideal structure for a wartime crisis. It was this crisis which gave birth to the Terror. It was not the Jacobin, but the Girondin-dominated Convention which had created the *représentants-en-mission*[2] to the provinces as well as the Revolutionary Tribunal on 9 March 1793; the same body which set up, on 21 March, those basic units of terror, the *comités de surveillance*,[3] and, on 7 April, the Committee of Public Safety. Furthermore, if one enquires into the origins of the revolutionary relationship between the central government and local municipalities and districts, one must look not to the Jacobins, but to the deputies of the Legislative Assembly, who, given the king's refusal to energise the entire nation for war, had instructed local government to set itself upon a war footing as early as the spring of 1792. The apparent contradiction between the Jacobin theory of liberal democracy—individual rights and the defence of property included—and the facts of the Terror cannot be resolved without reference to the facts of war and counter-revolution, which explains why [according to Anne Sa'adah] 'revolutionary Jacobinism preached the virtues of representative institutions and practiced the rigors of revolutionary government'.

What the Jacobins did possess, and the Girondins did not, however, was an unparalled network of clubs, radiating from the '*le club-mère*' in Paris to every corner of France, as well as to some of the major European cities. Michael Kennedy estimates that around 2 per cent of the French population was caught up in the Jacobin net, covering, as early as 1791, over 400 clubs. During the Terror, Jacobinism could create an alternative, 'unofficial' and revolutionary structure of government, headed by the *représentants-en-mission*, functioning through the Jacobin provincial clubs and operating alongside the thousands of *comités de surveillance* created in March by the Convention. At the apex of this 'Revolutionary Gov-

2. *Représentants-en-mission* were deputies who helped supervise the war effort in 1793.   3. The *comités de surveillance* were committees of revolutionary militants who made sure that revolutionary legislation was implemented.

ernment of the Year II' were the two great committees—the Committee of General Security, whose main jurisdiction was confined to police affairs, and the far more influential Committee of Public Safety, whose brief extended to every other aspect of government, military and civil. It must be remembered that the latter committee, composed of twelve deputies, including the 'triumvirate', Robespierre, [Louis] Couthon and [George-Auguste] Saint-Just, as well as very influential figures like [Lazare-Nicolas-Marguerite] Carnot (in charge of military affairs) and [Jean-Baptiste-Robert] Lindet (food supplies), was created by, and was ultimately responsible to, the National Convention. Robespierre would be overthrown inside, not outside, the Convention. Napoleon would first emasculate, then eliminate democratically elected national assemblies.

Problems Facing the Jacobins

The second major prop upon which the Jacobin Government of the Year II rested was the Popular Movement, particularly in Paris. It was a movement, unlike typical eighteenth-century 'crowds', which was organised and, even more important, armed. During the critical period of the summer of 1793 to the spring of the following year, the sansculottes, meeting nightly in draughty church halls draped with the appropriate revolutionary symbolism—tricolour flags, extracts from the Declaration of the Rights of Man, 'busts of the martyrs'—there at the dawning of their brave, new world, injected more revolutionary and martial vigour into the Republic's struggle for existence than any other socio-political group in the country. The forty-eight Sections of the capital—provincial towns had also been divided into Sections, ostensibly for electoral and administrative purposes—had been transformed, following their invasion by 'passive' citizens in the summer of 1792, into engines of political activity, each run by their own officials and committees, including the powerful *comités de surveillance*. Each of these forty-eight Sections sent two representatives to sit on the Paris Commune, but each Section, founded upon the life of the *quartier*, was jealous of its own powers. Not all of the Sections were radical; indeed, it was not until the autumn of 1793 that the radical Sections came to dominate the capital. The sansculottes, as these political activists proudly called themselves, took

the Constitution of 1793 seriously, and whether or not their political programme, which included the 'sovereignty of the people'
and the 'sacred right of insurrection', sprang from hand-me-down
versions of [philosopher Jean-Jacques] Rousseau or the require-
ments of a depressed artisanal and shopkeeper society, . . . they
came into increasing conflict with the Jacobin Government which,
whatever its own Rousseauesque pedigree, had a country to run
and two major wars, civil and foreign,[4] to win.

The Jacobin system of government, always intended as tempo-
rary, was forged in the white heat of revolution and war, tempered
by the internecine feuds within the Convention and the Paris
Commune, and packaged in a Rousseauesque wrapping of civic
and political *vertu*. The feuds within the Convention were provoked by the overall strategy of the Committee of Public Safety
which sought, initially, to harness the popular fury of the sansculottes against the enemies of the Republic, and then, when success
beckoned, to rein it in, a move prompted by the increasing fears
of the propertied elites. By the autumn of 1793, a period often described as the 'anarchic period of the Terror', the Parisian sansculottes had completed their defeat of the moderates in the Parisian
Sections and had launched a successful invasion of the National
Convention (4–5 September) which, reluctantly, granted them
legislation aimed at fixing the price of basic commodities (the Law
of the General Maximum) and the creation of a 'Revolutionary
Army', destined to become the striking force of the Terror in the
provinces. The forty or so *armées révolutionnaires* totalling some
40,000 volunteer ex-soldiers, artisans and craftsmen and spear-
headed by the Parisian *armée* led by Ronsin, provided the necessary sanction of force. Without it, the sansculottes argued, peasants and merchants would not empty their barns and warehouses
of goods, especially if they were obliged to take the increasingly
worthless *assignats* [paper currency introduced during the revo-
lution] as payment. More than any other single factor, it was these
armées which drove the Republic to the edge of anarchy during
the autumn and winter months of 1793–4, as they marched from
their urban bases out into the countryside to sell the message of

4. During 1792 and 1793 France was at war with Britain, Austria, and Prussia.

the sansculotte Revolution, more often than not to a bewildered, even hostile countryside. As Richard Cobb put it, the *armées*, for all the brevity of their existence,

> were 'essential cogs in the administration of the Terror; they represented the Terror on the move, the village Terror'. The *armées* came closest to realizing the dream of every sectionary militant—a guillotine on wheels, casting its long shadow over grain hoarders, counter-revolutionary priests, and foreign spies. . . .

Further Jacobin Difficulties

Gradually, the political and military circumstances for reining in the forces unleashed by mass popular involvement in the Revolution were being created. It is important to stress that Robespierre and the majority of his colleagues had always been uneasy about the more extreme members and policies of the Popular Movement: Robespierre was not the type of man who enjoyed a 'night with the boys' in the working-class *cabarets* of the faubourg Saint-Marcel: [Georges-Jacques] Danton, of course, would have been quite keen. The process of political disengagement from the Popular Movement may be said to have begun as early as August with Robespierre's denunciation of the *Enragé*[5] leader, Jacques Roux, who did know how the less fortunate members of society actually lived. On 9 September—just four days after the invasion of the Convention by the sansculottes it should be noted—the Parisian Sections were denied the right to sit *en permanence*. The sansculottes would trump this move by setting up their own popular societies in each Section, (the *sociétés sectionnaires*), underlining the fact that the Jacobin Government was still too weak to impose its will unchallenged. It could, however, strike at the women's movement which received scant support from the male chauvinist sansculottes. At the end of October, all clubs set up by women were closed, ending a very interesting and dangerous link between a putative form of feminism and the political extremism of the *En-*

5. *Enragés* were a small group of Parisian radical extremists who campaigned for strict economic controls.

ragés. It could also strike against common enemies: in the same month, Marie Antoinette and the leading Girondist deputies were executed.

The 'Triumvirate' of Robespierre, Couthon and Saint-Just experienced far more difficulty mastering the forces of opposition to the CPS [Committee of Public Safety] based in the Convention and the Paris Commune. Apart from a clutch of deputies tainted by corruption or links with foreign governments, there were two important factions opposing the Jacobin Government during the winter of 1793–94—the moderates in the Convention grouped around Georges Danton and Camille Desmoulins, and the extremists led by [Jacques-René] Hébert and [Pierre] Chaumette with their power base in the Paris Commune. The former should not be dismissed as unprincipled seekers after money and power: the Dantonists stood for an end to the Terror and a possible peace with Britain, representing a strand of opinion which links them to the Girondins. The Hébertists, on the other hand, represented that uncompromising call to arms on the part of the Popular Movement; increased Terror to defeat the foreigner abroad allied, and this is the important point, to a social policy directed at the 'selfish rich' at home. Throughout the month of November, Robespierre moved cautiously, denouncing extremism in all its forms, purging the Jacobin Club of 'foreign' plotters, particularly those involved in the dechristianisation campaign. During this period, Robespierre was the epitome of the careful politician, [according to David P. Jordan] 'the government man, who sees no difference between right and left, between *ultras* and *citras* as they were called: he saw only disequilibrium, crisis and competitors'.

CHAPTER 3

Social Change in Revolutionary France

Chapter Preface

The effects of the French Revolution went beyond that nation's borders. Within France new rights were being granted to previously neglected groups, among them the middle class, women, and Jews. Soon, France found one of its colonies seeking the same freedoms. Through the staunch fighting of its black soldiers and the leadership of Toussaint L'Ouverture, the colony of Saint-Domingue became Haiti, the first black republic, in 1804. Ironically, while Haiti remained independent from that point on, France was not so lucky—by 1804, the nation's first attempt at a republican government had failed and the nation was under the rule of self-proclaimed emperor Napoleon Bonaparte.

In 1789 Saint-Domingue was the largest of the French West Indian colonies. Five hundred thousand slaves, transported from Africa, worked on coffee, cotton, and sugar plantations. Since 1687 the slaves had lived under the Code Noir, or Black Code. Among the restrictions placed on slaves was that they had to be baptized into the Roman Catholic faith and could not gather with the slaves of other masters.

The inhabitants of Saint-Domingue were aware of the events of the French Revolution. Hearing news of the revolution inspired the aggrieved slaves, who staged a mass revolt on August 20, 1791. Plantation houses were set on fire, and slave masters were forced to flee. Emerging from the revolt as a key leader in the fight for independence was the self-educated slave Toussaint L'Ouverture. As Selden Rodman describes in his book *Haiti: The Black Republic*, Toussaint "was a small man and very homely, but shrewd and fearless and capable of inspiring a fanatical devotion among his followers."

In 1793 France went to war against Spain in an effort to gain complete control of the island (Spain owned part of the territory, which it had named Santo Domingo). Six hundred black soldiers joined the Spanish forces. However, the French troops, assisted by other slave soldiers, defeated the Spanish forces and took complete control of the island.

Toussaint was more successful in his next military effort. Great Britain invaded the island in September 1793 because it feared that a successful slave revolt could inspire a similar rebellion in its colony of Jamaica. Toussaint and Saint-Domingue's army fought the British forces until October 1798, when British troops withdrew after failing to subdue the slaves.

Spain and Britain no longer posed a threat to Saint-Domingue, but the colony had internal problems with which it now had to cope. Tim Matthewson explains in an article for *Military History Magazine:* "Slave revolts plunged the island into a chaos of internecine warfare between blacks, whites and the interracial mulatto populace that had become a separate class of its own. In 1800, however, Toussaint restored political order, and by 1802, slavery had ended in the colony." Rodman writes of Toussaint's efforts to draft a constitution for the island: "Toussaint neglected nothing to convince a hostile world that the first Negro state was prosperous, law-abiding and enlightened. But it was not to be."

France, now led by Napoleon Bonaparte, did not want to lose the wealth it had long enjoyed from Saint-Domingue's plantations. In 1802 Bonaparte sent his brother-in-law, Charles LeClerc, and forty-three thousand troops to fight against Toussaint's army. Bonaparte's call for a reinstatement of slavery made the island's troops even more eager to defeat the French invaders. According to Matthewson, "It was not the black and brown leaders who sparked this spontaneous rebellion; instead, it was the mid-level officers and lower ranks who seized the initiative."

In addition to withstanding the Saint-Domingue troops, the French army had to cope with an even deadlier enemy in yellow fever. By the time France surrendered on November 18, 1803, only seven thousand French soldiers had survived the fighting and illness. Sadly, Toussaint was not alive to see his dream fulfilled. On June 7, 1802, he was seized by LeClerc and sent to the French Alps. Toussaint fell ill and died ten months later. On January 1, 1804, Saint-Domingue military leader Jean Jacques Dessalines renamed the island Haiti and proclaimed its independence.

Haiti's fight for independence shows that the French Revolution had many consequences, both within France and beyond. In the following chapter the authors examine the ways the revolution transformed France. Few periods in history have led to more changes in such a relatively short amount of time.

Viewpoint 1

"Do you not believe, Gentlemen, that . . . wives and mothers of families could join together . . . to make [the constitution] loved?"

French Women Should Become Politically Active

Etta Palm d'Aelders

French women played an important role during the revolution. For example, on October 5, 1789, thousands of women marched to Versailles (the king's palace, twelve miles outside Paris) to protest the rising cost of bread; the king agreed to provide bread and returned to Paris with the protestors. Many women believed that they could contribute to the revolutionary government. One such woman was the Dutch activist Etta Palm d'Aelders. In the following viewpoint d'Aelders, who lived in France, details several of the ways French women could become involved politically. According to d'Aelders, patriotic women should provide assistance to young impoverished mothers. She also suggests that women supervise public education in order to ensure that French children are taught their rights and responsibilities. D'Aelders argues that allowing patriotic women to serve

Etta Palm d'Aelders, "Lettre d'une Amie de la Vérité," March 31, 1791.

in government will help foster in the general populace a love of country and respect for the new constitution.

M y fellow citizens, my brothers, if my feeble voice could reach your heart, if my zeal for the happiness of Frenchmen could inspire you to some extent, then listen to me. Rally around the tree of the constitution; it is the tree of life. Watch over the sacred fasces of the union; it is the bulwark of your liberty. Go, abjure on the altar of the Fatherland all hatred and partial enmity, all personal jealousies. Relegate to contempt, to anathema, whoever dares malign his brother; may love of the Fatherland, of liberty, of fraternity, be in your hearts as on your lips; let us all seek out ways of supporting one another, of succoring the unfortunate, of regenerating morals, of cherishing virtue, and of contributing, each of us, individually and in general, to making the French people the happiest people in the world. May your union and your happiness be blessed by all the nations.

In the eighty-three Departments,[1] armed citizens united to defend the constitution. Do you not believe, Gentlemen, that these wives and mothers of families could join together, following their example, to make it [the constitution] loved? The Société des amis de la vérité[2] is the first to have admitted us to patriotic sessions. Creil, Alais, Bordeaux [three bishops], and several others followed your example. Would it not be useful to form, in each Section[3] of the capital, a patriotic society of *citoyennes* [female citizens], female friends of the truth, whose general and federative circle would be supervised by you, Gentlemen, and would invite the fraternal societies of the eighty-three Departments to correspond with them. Each circle of *citoyennes* would meet in each Section as frequently as they believed useful for the public good and following their own particular rules; each circle would have its own

---

1. The National Assembly reformed France's local governments by dividing the nation into equal-size departments. These departments were then divided into districts, cantons, and communes (villages or towns), all of which were governed by elected local officials.   2. the Society of Friends of the Truth   3. the forty-eight units of local governments in Paris

directorate, which would meet once a week as a general staff under the supervision of the directorate of the friends of the truth. Thus, it would be in a position to supervise efficiently the enemies harbored in the midst of the capital and to differentiate the genuinely poor person in need of his brothers' aid from brigands called out by enemies. And the directorate of the central circle, corresponding with patriotic societies in the Departments, would propagate enlightenment and would make it possible to break up more easily the plots hatched by malevolent persons.

It is up to you, Gentlemen, friends of the truth, to develop the full utility of such an establishment. I would want to propose to my *concitoyennes* a means of demonstrating that they are worthy of the justice just rendered them by the august representatives of the nation; that they yield nothing to you in zeal for supporting your strengthening of their work.

Women's Clubs Would Be Valuable

These circles of women could be charged with overseeing the establishment of wet nurses. Ah! How urgent that a maternal view be taken of this administration, where a culpable negligence makes nature tremble. Yes, young women from the country, arriving in this huge capital without friends, without acquaintances, abandoned to themselves, without work and wandering around, prey to all kinds of seduction, often return home with their souls debased, their blood polluted. And innocent victims confided to these creatures are immolated or condemned to a painful existence and countless infirmities. A thousand other motives not any the less worthy of interest argue the necessity of a strict supervision of this administration to give healthy and robust men to a future generation.

Ah! Isn't this the field of honor where we must gather our laurels? These societies of *citoyennes* could be charged, in addition, with supervising public education. Wouldn't it be natural that charity schools, given over for the most part to ignorant people brought up with all kinds of prejudices, be under the immediate supervision of enlightened and virtuous *citoyennes*? Zealous women patriots would take care to teach children the rights of men, respect and obedience for the law, the duty of citizens, the decrees of the National Assembly,[4] and, finally, the revered names of France's regenerators instead of legends of the saints and the almanac of miracles.

These women's clubs could be charged in addition with investigating the conduct and the need of unfortunate people requesting aid from the Section—which would be easy, using the central circle where *citoyennes* from all the Sections would gather, because giving isn't everything, but giving well is. For example, a poor woman about to become a mother, deprived of all the assistance her condition calls for—doesn't she have sacred rights to our aid?

Woe to those among us who could look pitilessly upon their like, overwhelmed with misery, on a pallet of pain, bringing into the world an innocent victim whose cries, weakened by need, are calls for the preservation of life.

Woe to whoever, at the sight of this, does not share her clothing to cover her [the impoverished mother], and her necessities of life to aid her.

A Worthy Plan

Thus, by establishing a society of women in each Section, by means of a light contribution of a crown a month, a fund, for example, could be formed for indigent women (once expenses were deducted), and they could designate from their group a directress and commissioners charged with keeping a register of those who asked for their assistance.

These commissioners would be charged with going into humble dwellings to inform themselves concerning morals, conduct, or misfortunes of the indigent and with bringing consolation along with aid to their unfortunate brothers. In this way the distance between the rich and the poor would be narrowed infinitely. In this way charity would be excited in the one, courage and patience in the other. The morals of both would be purified and egoism destroyed, and the wealthy man, object of jealousy and envy, would become an object of love and veneration to his brother in indigence.

4. The name taken by a group of delegates from the Estates-General, a legislative body that was occasionally convened by the king. The National Assembly consisted of the representatives from the Third Estate (France's middle class and poor), along with some members of the clergy and aristocracy.

The Rights of French Women

Olympe de Gouges was one of the leading feminists of the French Revolution. In 1791 she wrote The Declaration of the Rights of Woman, *which was inspired by the seminal 1789 work* Declaration of the Rights of Man and Citizen. *In her declaration, de Gouges details what she believes are the political liberties and responsibilities of French women. The following is an excerpt from that document.*

Article I

Woman is born free and lives equal to man in her rights. Social distinctions can be based only on the common utility.

Article II

The purpose of any political association is the conservation of the natural and imprescriptible rights of woman and man; these rights are liberty, property, security, and especially resistance to oppression.

Article III

The principle of all sovereignty rests essentially with the nation, which is nothing but the union of woman and man; no body and no individual can exercise any authority which does not come expressly from it [the nation].

Article IV

Liberty and justice consist of restoring all that belongs to others; thus, the only limits on the exercise of the natural rights of woman are perpetual male tyranny; these limits are to be reformed by the laws of nature and reason.

Olympe de Gouges, *The Declaration of the Rights of Woman*, 1791.

This, Gentlemen, is a plan worthy of your attention. It is up to you, to the friends of the truth, to develop its full usefulness. I dare assure you that the courageous *citoyennes* who supported you with such passion in raising the altar of the Fatherland, on which you swore no longer to be anything other than a people of brothers, will applaud my project. Already they burn to show all Europe that if, when they were degraded under despotism, pleasing frivolity was their lot, then when they are restored to the dignity of their being, they will be the model for all civic virtues.

Citoyennes patriotes [patriotic citizens], to whom the august representatives of the nation have just given imprescriptible rights of nature of which a cowardly avidity, an unjust tyranny, deprived you, you no longer will be sacrificed to the avidity of a brother or immolated to your parents' pride. No longer will you be buried from the beginning of your existence in these odious caverns where you were forced to suffocate the heart's sweetest sentiments. No longer will it be a crime for you to be sensitive to the voice of nature.

Glory, immortal glory to the legislators of France, for having restored to the weakest but largest portion of humanity their rights—by decreeing equality of distribution [of properties]. But would it not be your duty to lay evidence of your gratitude at the feet of the august Senate which has just given you a civil existence?

A Formal Request

Therefore I make the formal motion that from among the women who are friends of truth, a deputation be named to go to the bar of the National Assembly to bear respectful and grateful witness before the representatives of France to what they just did for them and to promise these worthy fathers of the people that they will inspire their children with the same respect, the same love, for the constitution and the most ardent zeal in propagating moral and civil virtues.

Viewpoint 2

"A woman is only comfortable, is only in her place in her family or in her household."

French Women Should Remain in the Domestic Sphere

Louis Marie Prudhomme

In the following viewpoint Louis Marie Prudhomme contends that while French women might be needed to help fight the counterrevolution (a movement against the French Revolution led by loyalists to King Louis XVI), they ultimately belong in the domestic, not political, sphere. He asserts that although women are entitled to the rights of citizenship and free speech, they have never shown a great passion for civil and political liberty and are not suited for politics. Prudhomme maintains that women are only happy when they are taking care of their families and teaching morals to their children. Prudhomme was a bookseller during the revolution and the publisher of the radical newspaper *Revolutions of Paris.*

Many women have complained to us about the Revolution. In numerous letters they report to us that for two years now it

Louis Marie Prudhomme, "On the Influence of the Revolution on Women," February 12, 1791.

seems there is but one sex in France. In the primary assemblies [for voting], in the sections,[1] in the clubs, etc. there is no longer any discussion about women, as if they no longer existed. They are accorded, as if by grace, a few benches for listening to the sessions of the National Assembly [France's parliament]. Two or three women have appeared at the bar [spoken to the Assembly], but the audience was short, and the Assembly quickly passed on to the order of the day. Can the French people, some ask, not become free without ceasing to be gallant? Long ago, in the time of the Gauls, our good ancestors, women had a deliberative vote in the Estates of the nation; they voted just like men, and things did not go so badly. . . .

The reign of the courtesans precipitated the ruin of the nation; the empire of queens consummated it. We saw a prince [Louis XV], too quickly loved by the people, degrade his character in the arms of several women [his mistresses] without modesty, and become, following the example of [Babylonian king] Nebuchadnezzar, a brute who wallowed with a disgusting cynicism in the filth of the dirtiest pleasures. We saw his successor [Louis XVI] share with the public his infatuation with a young, lively, and frivolous princess [Marie Antoinette], who began by shaking off the yoke of etiquette as if practicing for one day shattering that of the laws. Soon following the lessons of her mother [Maria Theresa, empress of Austria], she profited from her ascendancy over little things to interfere in great ones and to influence the destiny of an entire people. . . .

The Functions of Each Sex

Solemn publicists have seriously proposed taking the road of conciliation; they have maintained that women enjoy the rights of citizenship like men and should have entry to all public assemblies, even to those that constitute or legislate for the nation. They have claimed that women have the right to speak as much as men.

No doubt, and this power has never been denied them. But nature, from which society should not depart except in spite of itself, has prescribed to each sex its respective functions; a house-

1. The forty-eight units of local governments in Paris. Run largely by devoted revolutionaries, they had judicial and administrative powers.

hold should never remain deserted for a single instant. When the father of a family leaves to defend or lay claim to the rights of property, security, equality, or liberty in a public assembly, the mother of the family, focused on her domestic duties, must make order and cleanliness, ease and peace reign at home.

Women have never shown this sustained and strongly pronounced taste for civil and political independence, this ardor to which everything cedes, which inspires in men so many great deeds, so many heroic actions. This is because civil and political liberty is in a manner of speaking useless to women and in consequence must be foreign to them. Destined to pass all their lives confined under the paternal roof or in the house of their marriage; born to a perpetual dependence from the first moment of their existence until that of their decease, they have only been endowed with private virtues. The tumult of camps, the storms of public places, the agitations of the tribunals are not at all suitable for the second sex. To keep her mother company, soften the worries of a spouse, nourish and care for her children, these are the only occupations and true duties of a woman. A woman is only comfortable, is only in her place in her family or in her household. She need only know what her parents or her husband judge appropriate to teach her about everything that takes place outside her home.

Guardians of Morality

Women! . . . The liberty of a people has for its basis good morals and education, and you are its guardians and first dispensers. . . . Appear in the midst of our national festivals with all the brilliance of your virtues and your charms! When the voice of the public acclaims the heroism and wisdom of a young citizen, then a mother rises and leads her young, beautiful, and modest daughter to the tribunal where crowns are distributed; the young virgin seizes one of them and goes herself to set it on the forehead of the acclaimed citizen. . . .

Citizenessess of all ages and all stations! Leave your homes all at the same time; rally from door to door and march toward city hall. . . . Armed with burning torches, present yourselves at the gates of the palace of your tyrants and demand reparation. . . . If the enemy, victorious thanks to disagreements between patriots, insists upon putting his plan of counterrevolution into action . . . you must avail yourself of every means, bravery and ruses, arms and poison; contaminate the fountains, the foodstuffs; let the atmosphere be charged with the seeds of death. . . . Once the country is purged of all these hired brigands, citizenesses! We will see you return to your dwellings to take up once again the accustomed yoke of domestic duties.

Viewpoint 3

"All men of whatever religion . . . must equally share the title and the rights of citizens."

French Jews Should Be Granted Citizenship

Jacques Godard

Approximately thirty thousand Jews lived in France (a mostly Catholic nation) when the French Revolution began. However, unlike Protestants—another religious minority—French Jews did not have the rights of citizens. For nearly two years the National Assembly, France's legislative body during the first stage of the revolution, debated the question of Jewish citizenship. On September 27, 1791, Jews were finally awarded the rights of citizens.

In the following viewpoint, excerpted from a petition delivered to the National Assembly on January 28, 1790, lawyer Jacques Godard argues in favor of citizenship. According to Godard, who writes on behalf of Jewish communities, Jews deserve citizenship because they have lived as French subjects and, therefore, should not be considered foreigners. He points out that because Jews have paid into the government in the form of taxes, just like other French subjects, they should enjoy the same advantages the government gives in return. Godard also argues

Jacques Godard, "A Petition to the National Assembly from Leaders of Jewish Communities," January 28, 1790.

that civil rights should be independent of religious beliefs and that no religious group should be permitted to oppress people of other faiths.

Let us begin with the principles that imperiously demand the elevation of the Jews to the rank of citizens.

A first principle is that all men domiciled in an empire, and living as subjects of that empire, must participate without distinctions in the same title and enjoy the same rights. They must all have the title and possess the rights of citizens.

Through being *domiciled*, in fact, and through their condition as *subjects*, they contract the obligation to serve the *patrie* [fatherland]; they serve it in reality; they contribute to the support of the public force: and the public force owes an equal protection and an equal distribution of benefits to all who unite to form it. It would be an extreme injustice if it did not render to all, in the same proportion, what it receives from all, and if some were favored by it to the prejudice of the others. These ideas do not need further development; their obviousness is evident to all minds.

Jews Are Not Foreigners

There is only one thing more to examine at this stage: are the Jews who live in France, or are they not, *domiciled* there? Do they or do they not live there as *subjects of France*?

Assuredly, it is unthinkable to regard them as foreigners; whether because they would be absolutely unable to assign themselves to another *patrie*; whether because they are born, become established, and have their families in France; whether because in certain cities they even have separate neighborhoods assigned to them; or whether, finally, because they pay all the taxes to which the French are subject, in addition to the other taxes that they are still made to pay separately.

Then Jews are therefore not *foreigners* in France. They are subjects of this empire; and consequently, they are and must be *citizens*. For in a State, whatever it be, one recognizes only two classes of men, *citizens* and *foreigners*. Those who are not in the second class must be in the first. The Jews, once again, are therefore and must be citizens.

Separating Religion and Civil Rights

In truth, they are of a religion condemned by that which is dominant in France. But the time is past when it was accepted that only the dominant religion gave the right to advantages, to prerogatives, to lucrative and honorable positions in society. For a long time this maxim, worthy of the Inquisition, was used against the Protestants; and the Protestants had no civil rights in France. Today, they have just been re-established in possession of civil rights; they are on the same footing as the Catholics in everything; the intolerant maxim that we have just recalled will no longer be applicable against them. Why should it continue to be used as an argument against the Jews?

In general, civil rights are entirely independent of religious principles. And all men of whatever religion, of whatever sect they may belong to, whatever form of worship they practice, provided that their cult, their sect, and their religion are not offensive to the principles of a pure and severe morality, all of these men, we say, since they can all equally serve the *patrie*, defend its interests, and contribute to its splendor, must equally share the title and the rights of citizens.

What would result from a contrary system, in virtue of which it would only be the single dominant religion, and others whose dogmas more or less resembled it, that could confer this title and these rights? The result would be the acceptance of the principle that force must prevail over weakness and the greater number over the lesser; whereas social rights must be calculated and measured only by justice.

The result would be that, in countries where it is not the Catholic religion that is dominant, the Catholics could be subjected legally to all the injustices with which the Jews are burdened today.

The result would be permission either to violate consciences or to seduce them. For you violate them by using persecution to force individuals to forswear their cults; you seduce them by offering them more advantages in the dominant religion than in their own. And you know that violence is no more permitted here than seduction. You know that in matters of belief it is to the evidence alone and not to force that man must submit his reason. You know that through force you would gain only indifferent people or hypocrites, and that in such conquests religion would have more to complain about than to applaud. You know, finally, that the Jew is attached to his religion, as you are to yours, and that injustices are no more permitted against him than they would be against you yourselves; that it is from itself and only itself that the conscience can receive its inspirations; that no being on earth has the right to command it; and that it is only God who can call men to account for their opinions relative to Him, and for the form under which they render homage to Him.

Tolerance Is Not the Answer

It will be permitted to the Jews to point out that no religion would have the right to assume dominion over another unless it could offer, in favor of the excellence of its origin, that irresistible evidence whose light must strike and convince all minds at the same time; but that, if it is impossible to assume that it has such evidence for all, it is equally impossible for it to be obligatory for all citizens; that, if it is impossible for it to oblige them all, then it is not a crime not to believe what it teaches; and that, if it is not a crime, there can be no penalty pronounced against those who refuse to submit to its dogmas.

And so the word *tolerance*, which, after so many centuries and so many *intolerant* acts, appears to be a word for humaneness and reason, is no longer suitable to a nation that wishes to affirm its rights on the eternal basis of justice. And America, to whom politics will owe so many useful lessons, has rejected it from its code as a term that tends to compromise individual liberty and to sacrifice certain classes of men to other classes.

To *tolerate*, in fact, is to suffer what one would have the right to prevent; and the dominant religion which, alone perhaps, as opposed to other religions, must have ministers recognized by the nation and a cult paid for by it, does not have the right to keep another from rising humbly beside it. Now the necessary consequence of this principle is that since different religions all have equal rights, it would be contradictory for there to be one of them which could give a right of pre-eminence over another, relative to the functions of citizens.

If one wishes to be even more convinced of this truth, let him reflect on the nature of these functions. They consist in paying to the State the taxes which are the price for tranquillity and for public safety; in defending the *patrie* as much in case of internal strife as in outside wars; in collaborating through the use of one's talents, intelligence, and virtues for the glory of the nation. Now in order to fulfill all these duties, is it necessary to be of one religion or another, to adopt or to reject this or that dogma? When men, united for the common defense, serve the public interest with equal ardor, are they going to be asked what they believe or what they do not believe? In a word, does anyone worry about the nature of their dogmas? Does it not matter more what they do than what they believe? Consequently, can their form of worship, whatever it is, be the measure of the rights that must be accorded them?

Thus, two incontestable principles assure the Jews the rights of citizens.

First, their qualification as *subjects of the kingdom* by itself assures them this right; we have proved it.

Their particular religion cannot deprive them of it; we have just established this.

Therefore it is a necessary consequence of true principles that they be declared citizens; and it is impossible that they not be so declared.

Viewpoint 4

"[France] cannot and should not admit to public posts, to the administration, . . . a tribe that, regarding itself everywhere as foreign, never exclusively embraces any region."

French Jews Should Not Be Granted Citizenship

Anne Louis Henri de la Fare

France had a population of 26 million in 1789, including thirty thousand Jews. Although Jews were allowed to practice their religion, they were not considered citizens. The National Assembly, France's legislative body during the first two years of the revolution, debated the issue of Jewish citizenship and awarded Jews full civil rights on September 27, 1791.

In the following viewpoint Anne Louis Henri de la Fare, the Bishop of Nancy, argues against citizenship for French Jews. La Fare asserts that Jews should not be granted the same rights as other inhabitants of France because Jews' customs are completely different from those of the rest of the nation and because Jews are not sufficiently attached to France. According to La Fare, Jews have sought a return to their homeland (Israel) since being expelled two thousand years earlier, first by the Babyloni-

Anne Louis Henri de la Fare, "Opinion on the Admissibility of Jews to Full Civil and Political Rights," Spring 1790.

ans and later by the Romans, and thus are unlikely to remain attached to any other nation. He also argues that although Jews are entitled to liberty and security, making them citizens could worsen prejudice against them.

Sirs, assure each Jewish individual his liberty, security, and the enjoyment of his property. You owe it to this individual who has strayed into our midst; you owe him nothing more. He is a foreigner to whom, during the time of this passage and his stay, France owes hospitality, protection, and security. But it cannot and should not admit to public posts, to the administration, to the prerogatives of the family a tribe that, regarding itself everywhere as foreign, never exclusively embraces any region; a tribe whose religion, customs, and physical and moral regime essentially differ from that of all other people; a tribe finally whose eyes turn constantly toward the common fatherland that should one day reunite its dispersed members and which cannot consequently consecrate any solid attachment to the land that supports it. . . .

There are only in France a small number of provinces where Jews have been permitted to establish themselves. The rest of the kingdom has but little or no relationship to the individuals of this nation. Thus, the greater part of the deputies would not know how to judge the present question with sufficient knowledge of the issue. The decision, nonetheless, is of a kind that should not be left to the enthusiasm of the emotions or to the seduction of the mind [presumably by excessively humanitarian leanings]. . . .

Preventing Future Violence

There are also moral and local consideration that should, if not guide, then at least enlighten the legislation regarding the Jewish nation.

The prejudices of the people against the Jews are only too well-known. From time to time, they explode into violence: recently in Alsace, some people committed the most criminal excesses against the Jews. A few months ago, similar misfortunes menaced them in Nancy [a city in Lorraine]. People wanted to pillage their houses, mistreat their persons; the animosity was extreme. Did they merit this malevolence because of criminal maneuvers, monopolies, or ventures contrary to the interests of the people? No, Sirs: the most serious reproach made to them was spreading out too much into the province, acquiring houses, lands, and privileges that the former laws did not give to them.

From this account it is easy to understand the habitual disposition of the people; it is a fire always ready to be lit. Any extension that a decree of the National Assembly [France's legislature] would hasten to give to the civil existence of the Jews, before opinion has been prepared in advance and led by degrees to this change, could occasion great disasters. It is only prudent to foresee possible misfortunes; it is only wise to prevent them.

Viewpoint 5

"Landowners, the bourgeoisie, bureaucrats, soldiers—all these groups did well out of the Revolution."

The French Revolution Transformed Many Elements of French Society

William Doyle

In the following viewpoint William Doyle asserts that although the French Revolution had some negative consequences, such as increased governmental intrusion into personal lives, it ulti-mately benefited much of French society. According to Doyle, groups who gained economic, political, and social power in-cluded property owners, soldiers, Jews, Protestants, and middle-class professionals. Doyle also notes that slaves in the French colony of Saint-Domingue benefited from the revolution. Civil rights proponents active in the revolution called for the abolish-ment of slavery in all French colonies, and the French govern-ment complied in 1794. Ten years later Saint-Domingue be-

William Doyle, *The Oxford History of the French Revolution*. Oxford, UK: Oxford University Press, 1989. Copyright © 1989 by William Doyle. Repro-duced by permission of the publisher.

came the independent nation of Haiti. Doyle is the chairman of the School of History at the University of Bristol in England.

W as . . . the Revolution worth it in material terms? For most ordinary French subjects turned by it into citizens, it cannot have been. It had made their lives infinitely more precarious, when they had expected the reverse. It had bidden fair to destroy the religious, cultural, and moral underpinnings of the communities in which they lived. The *cahiers* [letters] of 1789 make overwhelmingly clear that most French people wanted less state interference in their lives, yet it brought far more, and fiercer. Government by terror scarcely outlasted the Year II [September 1793 to September 1794], but nothing like it had ever occurred before. When it ebbed, the power of the State remained, permanently augmented and disposing of coercive powers not dreamed of by the old monarchy. It was no wonder therefore, that the most persistent and massive resistance that the Revolution encountered came not from the former so-called 'privileged orders' but from ordinary people who simply wanted to call a halt. In alienating so many of their fellow citizens, the revolutionaries furnished counter-revolutionaries with constant hope and encouragement. But most popular resistance was anti- rather than counter-revolutionary. Though they might mouth slogans about restoring Church and king, all most anti-revolutionaries wanted was stability and autonomy after years of upheaval and intrusion by outsiders. Their resistance, however, only too often pushed France's new authorities to further extremes of repression, gouging existing wounds yet wider and deeper.

Popular rejection of what the Revolution had become . . . was endemic throughout the south, where the Revolution was perceived as designed to benefit rich Protestants; and broke out periodically in rioting on local issues in many other areas. The statistics of emigration and terror are also suggestive. Almost 32,000, a third of all registered *émigrés*, were peasants or workers turning their backs on the land of liberty. Of the official victims of the Terror,[1] 8,350, or almost 60 per cent, were from the same groups, dying for their resistance. Deserters or draft-dodgers, tellingly defined as 'insubordinate' (*insoumis*), were another gauge. In 1789 drawing for the militia, one of the most hated institutions of the old order, had been abolished. By 1793 it was back, and in 1798 conscription assumed a far more systematic character. Evasion of military service was universally agreed to be a major ingredient in the rural crime wave which marked the directorial period. 'Many deserters are lurking about the woods', wrote an English traveller through Chantilly in 1796, 'and there are continual robberies and murders. We have not travelled half an hour in the dark.' Banditti, he called them later on: bandits—a category social scientists have learned to recognize as a classic form of protest against an established order. . . .

Yet some groups undoubtedly gained. In any list of them, pride of place must go to the owners of land. Freed in August 1789 from the burdens of feudalism and the tithe, they were able to proclaim property as the supreme social and political commodity. The Civil Code, when it was completed, consolidated and clarified their rights, and the means of transmitting them. Successive constitutions, in one way or another, made the effective exercise of political rights dependent in turn on property. Property would define the class of Notables who ruled France, as electors, from the Consulate down to the late nineteenth century. The social profile of property owners was little altered by the Revolution. The amount of land held by the nobility inevitably fell, although in the 1800s they still dominated the ranks of the largest and richest proprietors. At the other end of the scale the sale of national lands, especially in the mid-1790s when they had been marketed in small lots, had produced an increase in the number of petty peasant owners, though their overall share scarcely rose. The great gainers from the redistribution of church and noble property were the bourgeoisie. More than anything else, their fears about the security of their gains finally pushed the Revolution into the hands of a dictator [Napoleon] who imposed stability and offered all property owners unconditional recognition of their title. By the time he fell, their grip on their gains was beyond challenge, and the re-

1. between 1793 and 1794, when the radical Jacobin government authorized more than twenty thousand executions

stored Bourbons, though they returned *émigré* lands still unsold and organized a fund to compensate those whose property had gone, never seriously thought of undoing the land settlement bequeathed by the Revolution.

The bourgeoisie also gained by the Revolution, in the end, as the group from which the professions were recruited. The men of 1789 had proclaimed careers open to the talents, believing that neither birth nor wealth should give privileged access to any employment. At first the implementation of this principle looked like developing into a disaster for the professions. . . . The Revolution was early hostile to professional associations in general, interpreting their commitment to maintaining standards as a hangover from the now abandoned world of corporatism and privilege. 'This was one of the first abuses of freedom', recalled a distinguished lawyer, 'that the right was left to anyone, without scrutiny, or any apprenticeship, to practise the liberal professions.' Medicine, the bar, and the law in general were thrown open to the market, with minimal qualifications required from practitioners. Most of the former validating bodies, like universities, were abolished in any case. Revolutionary France was therefore a happy hunting ground for quacks and charlatans of every sort—most of them, to be sure, members of the bourgeoisie too. Not until Napoleonic times did the State take the situation in hand and reintroduce a rigorous system of licensing to restore professional standards. The solution was more bureaucratic than before 1789—but then so was France. . . .

Another group who did well out of the Revolution were soldiers. In no sphere were careers thrown more open to the talents, as the most successful careerist of them all was always ready to testify. Although military careers continued to attract high numbers of nobles still throughout the nineteenth century, the aristocratic monopoly of the officer corps had gone for ever. Proclaimed in 1789, equal opportunity in the army became a reality far more suddenly than could have been naturally expected when discipline collapsed and a large proportion of officers emigrated over the next two years. By 1793, accordingly, 70 per cent of officers in service had risen from the ranks. Even the officer-entry nobles who were left had their promotional chances improved by the departure of so many of their fellows. And for more than two decades after this, the vastly expanded army, first of the Great Nation, then of the Napoleonic Empire, would offer glory and good prospects to those who joined it and stayed with the colours. It was, of course, dangerous. By 1802 400,000 French men had fallen in battle, and another million, perhaps, would follow them before night fell on the field of Waterloo [site of Napoleon's final defeat]. The thousands of draft-dodgers and deserters who evaded each call-up showed clearly enough that the army's appeal was far from universal. Yet there was no mistaking the enthusiasm, commitment, and revolutionary arrogance of the Republic's armies. From the start soldiers were among the most fervent and extreme revolutionaries, scorning officers who still behaved like aristocrats, lynching generals suspected of treachery, cheering on dechristianization, and vigorously imposing the bracing discipline of liberty on defeated enemies. By 1795 and 1796, the opportunities for looting and plunder were limitless, and those lucky enough to be in the army of Italy had the unique privilege of being paid in coin. By 1797 the armies saw themselves in the former sansculotte[2] mantle as guardians of the Revolution's purity, standing ready to intervene in domestic politics under any successful general who would mouth slogans about saving the Republic from feckless babblers. When eventually the luckiest of such generals took power, military style was imposed on the State. . . .

Increased Religious Freedom

Landowners, the bourgeoisie, bureaucrats, soldiers—all these groups did well out of the Revolution, taking advantage of the circumstances it had brought about. Certain others benefited from deliberate and conscious acts of emancipation. Most prominent among them were the Protestants. Although the monarchy had been moving towards a more tolerant attitude with its grant of civil status in 1787, French Protestants welcomed the Revolution almost unanimously as their true benefactor, proclaiming as it did freedom of thought and worship and full equality of civil rights between all French citizens. They were quick to lay claim to these

2. Sansculottes were politically radical workers who wore long trousers, in opposition to the breeches worn by aristocrats.

rights, too—with inflammatory results in the cities of the south where old Catholic élites lost power as a result. Their triumph there merely confirmed their age-old reputation in Catholic eyes as subversives and troublemakers. Their early commitment did not save them in 1793 from the ravages of terror and dechristianization. . . . In the cities churches opened only a couple of years earlier (often in premises formerly the property of the Catholic Church) were closed or transformed into temples of reason. . . . Yet the annexation of Geneva in 1798 added the most famous Calvinist centre of all to French territory, and consular realism refused to countenance any return to Catholic legal dominance. In fact, under [Napoleon] Bonaparte, the Protestant churches were established on a parallel basis to the Catholic, with salaried pastors. . . . [By 1815,] there was no going back on the rights and status accorded to Protestants at the start of the Revolution, and confirmed by Bonaparte when he ended it.

The Revolution also brought emancipation to France's 39,000 Jews. Here again there had been signs of change before 1789. The name of [Henri] Grégoire first came to public notice when in 1784 he won the Academy of Metz's essay competition on the theme of how the lot of Jews could be improved. In the same year a number of legal disadvantages borne by the Jews of Alsace were lifted, and when the Revolution began the government was planning further concessions in what it, and Jewish leaders too, regarded as a natural corollary to the moves in favour of Protestants. Yet the National Assembly[3] proved in much less of a hurry to grant Jews the full rights of French citizens. When the issue was debated (which it was not until the last days of 1789) it became clear that many did not regard them as French at all. . . . Not until . . . 27 September 1791 were they admitted to full citizenship, against the vocal opposition of the Alsatian future Director, [Jean-François] Reubell. Strictly speaking, dechristianization could not be applied to Jews; but the practice of their religion was still persecuted in 1793 and 1794 by the Montagnard zealots of Alsace, who remembered that Jewish fanaticism and superstition were as much condemned by Voltaire

3. This was the name adopted by the Estates-General (a legislature that met occasionally in pre-Revolutionary France) during the early stages of Revolution.

and other prophets of progress as by undiminished popular prejudice. Prejudice remained when terror ended. . . . Not, however, until 1805 did the government intervene again in Jewish affairs, and then Napoleon's aim was to consolidate their position as citizens, if only by imposing closer state control on their activities. There was to be no return to the marginal status of before the 1780s—much to the disgust of the anti-Semites who continued to be found throughout French society.

Finally, reluctantly and belatedly, the Revolution also abolished slavery. In contrast to the case of Protestants and Jews, there was little expectation of change in this sphere before 1789. Although most of the *philosophes* had condemned slavery and the trade which sustained it, the first French abolition society, the Amis des Noirs, was not founded by Brissot until 1788. Only a handful of *cahiers* mentioned the issue, and the defenders of slavery were well organized and funded by the wealth of the colonial trade. They dominated the colonial committee of the National Assembly. But when the Assembly voted, in July 1789, to admit unconvoked deputies from Saint-Domingue [the Caribbean island originally called Hispaniola and now made up of the nations of Haiti and the Dominican Republic] did so only after a long and bitter debate about whom they represented. It had raised the question of the political rights of the numerous and increasingly well-organized free coloured population, not to mention the black slaves. And whereas, its decision made, the Assembly passed on to pressing metropolitan business, the impact on the colony itself was volcanic. Struggles for political control now began there between whites and free coloureds, culminating in an uprising of the latter in October 1790 which the whites put down with great brutality.

. . . News of these clashes provoked a new debate in Paris, and in May 1791 the Assembly, at the urging of deputies like Grégoire and [Maximilien] Robespierre, granted civil rights to coloureds born of two free parents. It was the Revolution's first gesture towards racial equality; but before news of it could reach Saint-Domingue, the slaves, stirred up by the ferocity of the political conflicts around them, had risen in the great rebellion of August 1791. It was the progress of this uprising that forced the pace on racial issues. In April 1791 the Legislative, of which [Jacques-Pierre] Brissot was the most prominent member, granted full rights to all free coloureds regardless of parentage. But when commissioners sent out to enforce the new law arrived in the colony, they found the situation so envenomed that it made little impact. Within months of their arrival, France was at war with Great Britain, and communications with home perilous. Willy-nilly the commissioners were forced to use their own initiative in responding to a complex and shifting situation. Thus . . . by the beginning of February 1793 Commissioner [Leger Felicite] Sonthonax was beginning to denounce 'aristocrats of the skin'. The latter responded by trying to drive the commissioners from the colony by force. Only nonwhites defended Sonthonax, and in recognition of this in June 1793 he offered freedom to all blacks who would fight for the Republic. 'It is', he declared, 'with the natives of the country, that is, the Africans, that we will save Saint-Domingue for France.' Two months later, as Spaniards from the other part of the island invaded the troubled colony, he took the final step. On 29 August, slavery itself was abolished in the northern province. In October general freedom was proclaimed for all Saint-Domingue. None of this had been authorized by the Convention. . . . But when news of the emancipation arrived in Paris in January 1794 the Convention greeted it with enthusiasm, if only because, like Sonthonax, the deputies saw it as a way to defeat the Republic's British and Spanish enemies in the Caribbean. On 4 February, accordingly, the Convention framed its own decree: Negro slavery was abolished in all French colonies, and all men living there were citizens with full rights.

The effect was dramatic. As soon as the news arrived in the colony, late in April, black rebel leaders began to rally to the Republic. The free black Toussaint L'Ouverture, who had joined the Spanish invaders, switched sides. The Spaniards were driven out by black forces, who proceeded to massacre whites who had welcomed the invaders. Under the peace of 1795 Spain ceded all of Hispaniola to France. . . . Slavery lasted . . . in French colonies down to 1848. But it was never re-established in Saint-Domingue, which proclaimed itself, on 1 January 1804, the Republic of Haiti. . . .

French control over the former richest colony in the world was never regained. Haiti was thus the only truly independent state to come into being as a result of the French Revolution.

Viewpoint 6

"The 'modern men' who seemed poised to capture government under Louis XVI . . . resumed their march to power once the irritations of revolutionary politics were brushed aside."

The French Revolution Did Not Transform French Society

Simon Schama

In the following viewpoint Simon Schama asserts that the French Revolution did not significantly transform that nation's society. According to Schama, the landed classes remained wealthy while the rural poor made virtually no economic advances. He also notes that the revolutionary governments did not solve the financial problems that had been associated with the monarchy. Schama concludes that upon Napoleon's declaration in 1799 that the revolution had ended, the men who were poised to take power prior to 1789 were able to resume their march to power. Schama is a professor of history at Columbia University in New York City and the author of *Citizens: A*

Chronicle of the French Revolution, the source of the following viewpoint.

Was the world of the village in 1799 so very different from what it had been ten years before? In particular regions of France where there had been heavy emigration and repression, rural life had indeed been emptied of noble dominance. But this obvious rupture disguises a continuity of some importance. It was exactly those sections of the population who had been gaining economically under the old regime that profited most from the sale of noble and church lands. Those sales were declared irreversible, so there was indeed a substantial transfer of wealth. But much of that transfer was *within* the landed classes—extending from well-to-do farmers up to "patriot" nobles who had managed to stay put and actually benefited from the confiscations. Fat cats got fatter. In Puiseux-Pontoise in the Seine-et-Oise, the Marquis de Girardin's biggest tenant and neighbor, Charles-Antoine Thomassin, was well positioned to snap up available lots and did so well that he competed with his former landlord for any remaining parcels. There were, to be sure, many regions of France where the nobility as a group lost a considerable part of their fortune. But there were also others—in the west, the center and the south—where, as Jean Tulard has shown, lands that remained unsold could be recovered by families who returned in substantial numbers after 1796. Thus, while many of the leading figures in this history ended their lives on the guillotine, many others stayed put and reemerged as the leading notables of their department. The callow young *maître de cérémonies* who wilted before [political leader Honoré Gabriel Riquetti, count of] Mirabeau's wrath on June 23, 1789, the Marquis de Dreux-Brezé, was still the fourth richest man in the department of the Sarthe during the Consulate and Empire. Barral de Montferrat, the ex-president of the Parlement of the Dauphiné who became mayor of Grenoble during the Revolution, remained one of the great powers of the Isère well into the nineteenth century. In the Eure-et-Loir the Noailles family remained the great landed dynasty; in the Oise, the Rochefoucauld-Liancourts were still among

the greatest proprietors, notwithstanding the disasters that had be-
fallen the citizen-nobles of the clan.

Few Gains for the Poor

By contrast, the rural poor gained very little at all from the Revolution. Saint-Just's Ventôse laws[1] remained a dead letter and it became harder than ever to pasture animals on common land or
gather fuel from the open woods. In all these respects the Revolution was just an interlude in the inexorable modernization of
property rights that had been well under way before 1789. No government—that of the Jacobins any more than that of the King—
had really answered the cries for help that echoed through the rural *cahiers de doléances* [letters of grievance] in 1789.

Likewise, the brutal rupture of religious continuities under the
Terror[2] was only a passing phenomenon—though never forgotten in the villages. Liberty hats that had replaced crosses on spires
and towers were abruptly removed and destroyed in the year III
[September 1794 to September 1795]. The cult of the Supreme
Being gradually gave way to open profession of the old faith, often pressed by women, who, in many parts of France, embarked
on an angry campaign of reconsecration, forcing juring priests to
scrape clean the tongue of anyone who had been polluted by a
constitutional communion. Bells began to chime again over the
fields and cottages and traditional festivals were restored, even if
they had to be celebrated in Nivôse and Germinal rather than December and April.

Had the Revolution, at least, created state institutions which resolved the problems that brought down the monarchy? Here, too,
as [nineteenth-century historian Alexis] de Tocqueville empha-
sized, it is easier to discern continuities, especially of centralization,
than any overwhelming change. In public finance, the creation of
a paper currency came to be recognized as a catastrophe beside
which the insolvencies of the old regime looked almost picayune.
Eventually the Bonapartist Consulate (whose finances were ad-

1. Under the Ventôse laws, devised by revolutionary Louis de Saint-Just, needy
citizens would share seized property.   2. between 1793 and 1794, during the
rule of the radical Jacobin government, when more than twenty thousand people
were executed

ministered overwhelmingly by surviving bureaucrats of the old regime) returned to a metallic system based on [Charles Alexandre de] Calonne's important monetary reform of 1785 fixing the ratio of silver to gold. Fiscally, too, post-Jacobin France slid inexorably back to the former mixture of loans and indirect as well as direct taxes. The Republic and Empire did no better funding a large army and navy from these domestic sources than had the monarchy and depended crucially on instutionalized extortion from occupied countries to keep the military pump primed.

A Brutal but Brief Interruption

The Napoleonic prefects have always been recognized as the heirs of the royal *intendants* (and the revolutionary *représentants-en-mission*),[3] brokering administration between central government priorities and the interest of the local notability. Without any question that notability had suffered a violent shock during the height of the Jacobin Terror, especially in the great provincial cities, where, after the federalist revolt, they were virtually exterminated. The constitution of the year III, however, with its reintroduction of tax qualifications for the electoral assemblies, returned authority to those who had, in many places, exercised it continuously between the mid-1780s and 1792. As we have seen, in some small towns, such as Calais, where adroit mayors paid lip service to passing regimes, there was unbroken continuity of office from 1789 through to the Restoration. Looking at the department of the Orne, Louis Bergeron has found an extraordinary degree of continuity in the notability, whether measured by income, status or office. Goupil de Prefeln, for example, had been a *conseiller du Parlement* at Rouen and deputy to the Constituent, and became *procureur-général* of the Napoleonic court at Caen in 1812. Descorches de Sainte-Croix, who had been *maréchal de camp* in the old royal army, was now a prefect and baron of the Empire. For these men and countless others like them, the Revolution had been but a brutal though mercifully ephemeral inter-

---

3. *Intendants* were the main agents of the crown in the provinces under the Old Regime. *Représentants-en-mission* were deputies who helped supervise the war effort in 1793.

ruption of their social and institutional power.

The Dictatorship of Virtue had also threatened the growing orthodoxy in the reign of Louis XVI according to which public officials ought to have a modicum of professional expertise, and at high levels should make full use of the "modern" professions: engineering, chemistry, mathematics. The great exponent of a state in which science and virtue would be mutually reinforcing, the Marquis de Condorcet, died in abject defeat, escaping from house arrest in Paris in May 1794 and walking all the way to Clamart only to arouse suspicion at an inn when he ordered an omelette. "How many eggs?" asked the *patronne*. "Twelve," replied Condorcet, suggesting a damaging unfamiliarity with the cuisine of the common man. He was locked up for the Revolutionary Tribunal but was found dead in his cell before he could be transported to Paris. A choice of legends is available to explain the disaster: exhausted starvation or the more glamorous end of poison

Permanent Elements in French Society

If . . . we look with all open mind on the society that emerged from the revolution, we will be most struck by the permanent elements in the French social pattern. We will see a society with many new elements it is true, but bearing on it like a palimpsest the inadequately effaced writing of the *ancien régime*. The whole development of French society appears in a different light if we recognise that the revolution was a triumph for the conservative, propertied, land-owning classes, large and small. This was one of the factors—of course not the only one—contributing to the economic backwardness of France in the following century. It helps us to see that in the course of the revolution the social hierarchy, modified and based more openly on wealth, particularly landed wealth, and political influence, and less on birth and aristocratic connections, was strengthened and reasserted.

Albert Cobban, *The Social Interpretation of the French Revolution*, 1965.

taken from a ring. If the latter is true, it would have been in keeping with the rage for suicide that swept through the Girondins after their proscription.

Though the author of the *Esquisse du Progrès Humain* (The Sketch of Human Progress) had perished, the intellectual elite of the academies continued the colonization of government they had begun in the reign of Louis XVI. The great reforms of higher education that embodied the thought of the late Enlightenment took place under the Directory with the creation of the *écoles centrales* [central schools]. And the world of the *musées* [museums] and academies in both Paris and the provinces resumed its intellectual energy free from political intimidation (though not from infighting, since that is in the nature of the beasts) during the 1790s. The councils of state and ministries under the Consulate and Empire[4] were filled with the intellectual eminences of the 1780s. Some had been, en route, ardent revolutionaries; some had not. [Jean Antoine] Chaptal, the royal inspector of mines and professor of chemistry, ennobled by Louis XVI in 1788 on the usual meritocratic ladder, became a Napoleonic minister of the interior. Charles Gaudin, the Minister of Finance, was the son of a Parlementaire lawyer who had worked for the administration of the *vingtième* tax before 1789. Two ministers of justice, Abrial and Regnier, had both likewise been Parlementaires before the Revolution, had public careers early in the Revolution, survived the Terror and sailed on to power and status in the Directory and Consulate.

Creating a New Government

What killed the monarchy was its inability to create representative institutions through which the state could execute its program of reform. Had the Revolution done any better? On one level, the succession of elected legislatures, from the Estates-General to the National Convention, was one of the most impressive innovations of the Revolution. They took the intensive debate on shape of governing institutions in France, which had been going on for at least

4. The Consulate was the government established after the coup of 18 Brumaire; Napoleon Bonaparte was one of the three consuls. He eventually gained complete control and named himself emperor of France.

half a century, into the arena of representation itself and articulated its principles with unparalleled eloquence. But for all their
virtues as theaters of debate, none of the legislatures ever managed
to solve the issue that had bedeviled the old regime: how to create
a viable working partnership between the executive and the legislature? Once the Constituent had rejected [Jean-Joseph] Mounier
and Mirabeau's "British" proposal of drawing ministers from the
assembly, it regarded the executive not as the administration of
the country, working in good faith, but as a fifth column bent on
subverting national sovereignty. With this doomed beginning, the
executive and legislative branches of the constitution of 1791 simply intensified the war with each other until their mutual destruction in 1792. The Terror effectively reversed matters by
putting the Convention under the thrall of the committees, but
still made it impossible to change governments except by violence.

The framers of the constitution of the year III (1795) obviously
learned something from this unhappy experience. A two-chamber
legislature was introduced, elected indirectly from colleges in
which property was the criterion for membership. A governing
council was in theory accountable to the legislature (as indeed the
committees had been). In practice, however, the experiment remained darkened by the long shadow of the Revolution itself, so
that factions inevitably crystallized, not around specific issues of
government but plans for the overthrow of the state, hatched either by royalists or neo-Jacobins.[5] With the separate organs of the
constitution in paralyzing conflict with each other, violence continued to determine the political direction of the state far more
than did elections.

But the violence was, after the year III, no longer coming from
the streets and *sections* but from the uniformed army. If one had
to look for one indisputable story of transformation in the French
Revolution, it would be the creation of the juridical entity of the
citizen. But no sooner had this hypothetically free person been invented than his liberties were circumscribed by the police power

---

5. Neo-Jacobins were a radical political group who formed in the latter years of
the revolution, several years after the original Jacobins, including Maximilien
Robespierre, had been overthrown.

of the state. This was always done in the name of republican patriotism, but the constraints were no less oppressive for that. Just
as Mirabeau—and the [Maximilien] Robespierre of 1791—had
feared, liberties were held hostage to the authority of the warrior
state. Though this conclusion might be depressing, it should not
really be all that surprising. The Revolution, after all, had begun
as a response to a patriotism wounded by the humiliations of the
Seven Years' War. It was [Charles Gravier, count of] Vergennes'
decision to promote, at the same time, maritime imperialism con-
tinental military power which generated the sense of fiscal panic
that overcame the monarchy in its last days. A crucial element—
perhaps, indeed, *the* crucial element—in the claim of the revolutionaries of 1789 was that they could better regenerate the *patrie*
than could the appointees of the King. From the outset, then, the
great continuing strand of militancy was patriotic. Militarized nationalism was not, in some accidental way, the unintended consequence of the French Revolution: it was its heart and soul. It was
wholly logical that the multimillionaire inheritors of revolutionary power—the true "new class" of this period of French history—
were not some *bourgeoisie conquérante* [middle-class conquerors]
but *real* conquerors: the Napoleonic marshals, whose fortunes
made even those of the surviving dynasts of the nobility look pal-
try by comparison.

For better or worse, the "modern men" who seemed poised to
capture government under Louis XVI—engineers, noble indus-
trialists, scientists, bureaucrats and generals—resumed their
march to power once the irritations of revolutionary politics were
brushed aside. "*La tragédie, maintenant, c'est la politique,*" ["Politics are now the tragedy"] claimed Napoleon, who, after the coup
d'état that brought him to power in 1799, added his claim to that
which had been made by so many optimistic governments before
him, that "the Revolution is completed."

CHAPTER 4

Historians Evaluate the French Revolution

Chapter Preface

While unquestionably important, the French Revolution was not the seminal event of the eighteenth century in the minds of many American historians. Indeed, in their view, the American Revolution enjoys that honor. In 1775 the American colonies began their fight for independence from Great Britain. By the summer of 1789, when France's middle and lower classes first threatened the monarchy, the newly formed United States had already written a constitution and elected its first president. A dozen years later the United States had peacefully elected its third president, while France—whose initial attempt at a republic did not survive its seventh year—had fallen under the dictatorship of Napoleon Bonaparte. Although many modern historians have looked at the two revolutions as complementary facets of an "Atlantic Revolution," American writers and observers in the eighteenth and nineteenth centuries tended to separate the two events, believing the French Revolution a failure that should not be considered equal to the American triumph.

Americans widely supported the French Revolution during its early years. They saw in the French kindred spirits, men and women who were eager to earn political and civil rights. However, by 1792 the United States began to doubt the path that France's revolutionary leaders had taken. Maximilien Robespierre and his Jacobin brethren had taken over the government and started to oppress their moderate and conservative opponents; Jacobin rule may be best remembered for the Reign of Terror, when more than twenty thousand Jacobin opponents, including the former king Louis XVI and his wife Marie Antoinette, were executed. For many Americans it was the Jacobin's treatment of the Marquis de Lafayette that made them turn against the French cause.

Lafayette was a beloved figure in America. The French noble and Royal Army officer had arrived in South Carolina on June 13, 1777, to lend his support to the colonial army. He proved himself essential to the revolutionary struggle, serving as a major general alongside George Washington in the Battle of Brandywine and at the army's winter quarters in Valley Forge. Lafayette returned to France in October 1778, where he successfully petitioned the French government to send troops and supplies to the struggling young nation and also spent his own money on supplies. He returned to America in April 1780 and helped lead the forces that won the final victory against the British at Yorktown.

Given Lafayette's popularity in the United States, it is not surprising that Americans were upset to learn in 1792 that Lafayette, who was by then leading the French army in a war against Austria, had been forced to flee to Belgium when the Jacobins took over the government. Lafayette was captured by the Austrians and turned over to the Prussians, who imprisoned him until 1797. Even after his release, Lafayette was unable to return to France till 1800. Americans, upset by France's treatment of Lafayette and by the atmosphere of violence in France, were eager to separate themselves from what had once been looked upon as a sister revolution. In an article for *The History Teacher*, Casey Harison, a history professor at the University of Southern Indiana, writes:

> The American inclination to distinguish the two [revolutions] had begun early in the nation's history. . . . For example, John Quincy Adams remarked in 1800 that an essay he was reading was worthy of publication because it (the essay) 'rescu(ed)' the American Revolution from the disgraceful imputation of having proceeded from the same principles as the French.

These eighteenth-century attitudes spilled over into nineteenth-century interpretations of the French Revolution from the American perspective. Among the examples of history texts giving a negative view of the revolution is Joseph Worcester's 1835 book *Elements of History*. According to Harison, Worcester "[sympathized] with some of the early events of the French Revolution. . . . The start of the Revolution is characterized as representing 'progress.' . . . Lafayette especially is given a prominent role, and his abandonment of the Revolution is construed as the moment when events shift from praiseworthy to troubling." Harison further argues that these negative historical interpretations had several other causes. For example, nineteenth-century America was an overwhelmingly Protestant nation that tended to look askance at largely Catholic France. In addition, suggests Harison, "The most likely explanation for the predominance of negative views of the French Revolution . . . is the influence of Thermidorean (that is, French counterrevolutionary) or hostile English interpretations." One of those English interpretations had come from British political theorist and orator Edmund Burke. In the 1770s he supported the American Revolution, contending that it was a necessary response to a tyrannical king. By comparison, in his 1790 publication, *Reflections on the Revolution in France*, Burke asserted that those who started the French Revolution had acted irrationally against a lawful monarch.

A more positive view of the revolution, one that sees similarities between the two revolutions, has emerged in recent decades. However, the French Revolution is still not looked upon by American historians as an unequivocally beneficial event. In the following chapter historians debate whether the French Revolution can be considered a success or a disappointment. Undoubtedly, the consequences of the events of eighteenth-century France, whether ultimately good or bad, helped change the course of the past two centuries.

Viewpoint 1

"The Revolution undoubtedly aggravated the recession of the 1780s."

The French Revolution Had Largely Negative Effects on the Economy

Gwynne Lewis

France's economic woes under Louis XVI have often been cited as causing the French Revolution. However, as Gwynne Lewis asserts in the following viewpoint, the revolutionary government did little to improve the nation's economic situation. Although Lewis acknowledges that some industries, notably cotton and iron, flourished during the revolution, and she concedes that France began to take steps toward modern capitalism, she argues that the revolution worsened the preexisting recession. According to Lewis, the value of France's overseas trade was reduced by half between 1789 and 1799 while the textile and coal industries also experienced losses and stagnation. She notes that hyperinflation and war led the nation to further economic disarray. Lewis is a professor of history at the University of Warwick in Coventry, England, and the author of *The French Revolution: Rethinking the Debate*, the source of the following viewpoint.

[H]istorian] Florin Aftalion believes that '. . . the return of a degree of economic liberty allowed the French economy to recover slowly from the shock of the Revolution'. The shaky recovery after 1795 may be explained by many other factors, including the creation of a French empire in Europe, offering not only plunder in cash and kind, but new markets for French goods, denied access to British and most colonial ports. But what was the state of the French economy as the 1790s drew to its bloody end? How had the Revolution affected French agriculture, industry and overseas trade? So far as the last is concerned, the answer is unequivocal—it had been a disaster. Between 1789 and 1799, France's external trade probably halved in value, the trade with America and the colonies being dealt an even more severe blow. Free-trade principles had never been applied in the French colonies; they were, as was the case with the English, for home consumption only. On 21 September 1793, the Convention had passed the Navigation Act, in the vain attempt to ensure that all goods were carried in French ships. The problem was that there were fewer goods to carry, the war with England, allied to upheavals in French colonies, having ruined the lucrative re-export trade. This spelled, if not disaster, then serious problems for the Atlantic and Mediterranean ports of Marseille, Bordeaux and Nantes. Saint-Domingue, the 'jewel in the crown' so far as France's colonial trade in the eighteenth century was concerned, was lost as the first great black revolt in modern times, led by Toussaint Louverture, destroyed the bases of the old planter economy. Again, however, we need to note that France's trade with her colonies, particularly in manufactured goods, had been declining since the late 1770s.

Changes in Trade and Industry

To get things really in perspective we need to look at the broader canvas. The Revolution redirected French trade and industry along

lines which followed the general switch of trade from a 'Mediterranean' to an 'Atlantic' economy. One can detect a relationship
here between the decline—though certainly not the death—of the
old 'proto-industrial' textile products such as linen and wool,
based mainly in the south and west, and the rise of the newer industries such as cotton, coal and iron, as well as the chemical industries which were based, again mainly, in the north and east of
France. In order to present a balanced picture of the impact of the
Revolution upon French trade and industry, we must return to
this issue of long-term structures and place the developments of
the 1790s within the longer time-sequence. The existence of traditional, 'proto-industrial' methods of production, which fitted
snugly into a predominantly rural and seigneurial [feudal] society, represents one of the most obvious but often neglected brakes
upon the growth of modern French capitalism. France's economic
growth in the eighteenth century, particularly in the textile industry, had occurred within the old proto-industrial economy, that is
an economy run by family 'peasant-artisans', based upon small,
often domestic, units of production, but producing for national
and international markets. These older sectors of the economy
were badly affected by the Revolution. Typical of the proto-industrial mentality was the case of the inhabitants of Longwy in the
north-east of France who demanded in their *cahier de doléances*
[letters of grievance] in 1789 that iron-masters should only be allowed to use wood after 'the local inhabitants had taken what they
wanted'. Or take the case of one of the most dynamic and gifted
entrepreneurs in eighteenth-century France, Pierre-François
Tubeuf. His attempt to concentrate and modernise the scores of
small coal-mines in the Alès region of south-eastern France was
defeated by the combined efforts of a *grand seigneur* [feudal lord],
the marquis de Castries, and the bitter and violent resistance of
hundreds of proto-industrial coal-miners, textile-workers, char-
coal and lime-burners, eager to protect their independence and
traditional way of life from the incursions of modern capitalism.
Tubeuf, ruined by debt, eventually emigrated to America, there to
die at the hands of 'les Peaux Rouges' [Native Americans], also
vainly trying to protect a traditional socio-economic system.

The Revolution undoubtedly aggravated the recession of the

1780s, reinforcing, in many ways, the proto-industrial mentality of peasants who divided their time between agricultural work in the spring and summer and making textiles in the late autumn and winter. The massive sale of National Lands meant that land, rather than trade or industry, became even more attractive as a source of investment. War, with its insatiable demand for men, food and animals, hyper-inflation and then the terrible winter of 1794 further disrupted the economy, so that by 1795–6 overall industrial production had reached its lowest point since 1789, possibly a drop of two-thirds. Lyon, pride of the French silk industry, was seriously affected by the bloody civil war which had raged in its streets since 1793, helping to account for a 50 per cent drop in production.

Signs of Growth

But there were growth sectors, providing the nuclei of modern industrial capitalism. The cotton industry developed new techniques, particularly in the printed cotton sector: Fontaine-Guérard had invested 300,000 *livres* in his cotton ventures in the Eure department by 1792; Oberkampf had placed a similar sum in his Jouy-en-Josas works between 1790 and 1793. Imports of raw cotton rose from 4,800 tonnes in 1789 to 7,000 by 1803. At Rouen, 19,000 kilogrammes of printed cloth had been produced in 1789, 32,000 by 1800. The metallurgical industry obviously benefited from the war. Cast-iron production more than doubled, from 50,000 *tonnes* to 120,000, between 1789 and 1800; although the number of blast furnaces fell from 600 to 500 in the same period, capacity increased indicating, as in the cotton sector, some technological innovation. On the other hand, coal production remained static at around 750,000 *tonnes.*

Revisionist historians, from Alfred Cobban to Emmanuel Le Roy Ladurie, have rightly insisted that, if one looks at the statistics of industrial or agricultural growth, or the substantial increase in the size of the small-scale farming sector, the French Revolution can in no way be described as a 'capitalist revolution'. They are surely right to insist that, certainly when compared with their great rival England, the period from 1789 to 1815 was, to put it at its best, a period of economic stagnation. *Marxisant* historians accept that there was little growth in the key industrial and agricul-

tural sectors of the economy, although Albert Soboul, for example, would stress the fact that, in the cotton industry for one, there
was significant technological and structural change. But their argument rests more upon the revolutionary consequences of the
abolition of feudalism, the declining influence of the Catholic
Church (opposed to usury), the abolition of the guilds, the introduction of anti-combination laws such as the Loi Chapelier of
1791, of the metric system, of a standardised system of weights
and measures, of the shift from traditional, communitarian to
modern contractual relationships between peasants and landlords,
managers and workers. In other words, from a legal and juridical
standpoint, France had taken a major, if not a giant, step on the
road to a modern capitalist society. When evaluating the failure
to match England's impressive spurt in those industries which
were to be the sinews of a modern industrial society, such as coal
and cotton, during the revolutionary and Napoleonic period, due
attention has to be paid to the relatively massive peasant sector of
France's economy before 1789 as well as to the extent of proto-
industrial forms of manufacturing production. The sale of huge
tracts of Church and *émigré* lands would undoubtedly retard the
development of modern forms of industrialisation, if only by
soaking up much-needed investment funds. This fact provides
one of the major explanations for the slow pace of French industrialisation, when compared, as it invariably is, with the British
model. Finally, one needs to ask how many investors would be inclined to put their money into risky industrial ventures during a
period of war and instability which would last for over twenty
years? The political economy of the revolutionary and Napoleonic
period was, after all, a war economy. Grandiose notions of laissez-
faire economics soon collapsed on the battlefields of Europe and
the sealanes to the colonies.

Viewpoint 2

"[The Jacobins] proved that democracy restores finances, while the big bourgeoisie throws them into disorder."

The French Revolution Had Positive Effects on the Economy

Jacques Solomon

Jacques Solomon, a French physicist and socialist who was executed by the Nazis during World War II, praises the economic policies of Maximilien Robespierre and the rest of the Jacobin leadership in the following viewpoint. Solomon asserts that these radical revolutionaries saved France from the dangers posed by foreign invaders and counterrevolutionaries while also stabilizing the French currency. According to Solomon, the Jacobins compelled France's wealthy subjects to contribute money to support the revolution and the disadvantaged. He also contends that the new government greatly benefited France by stabilizing the paper currency, *assignats*, by reducing the circulation of money, establishing an official exchange rate, and setting

Jacques Solomon, "The Finances of the Revolution," *Essays on the French Revolution*, edited by T.A. Jackson, translated by William Zak. London: Lawrence and Wishart, 1945.

maximum prices that made bread and other provisions affordable without completely eliminating commercial profits.

[M]aximilien] Robespierre and his friends succeeded in saving France from counter-revolutionary foreign invaders,
despite revolts fomented by the agents of the aristocracy and foreign Powers, and made the currency more stable than before. Let
us examine the method of this remarkable and rarely-recognized
financial success.

The First Victory

Firstly, despite the Girondins, the Jacobins raised a forced loan of
1,000 millions.[1] The law of May 20th, 1793, prescribed: "There
shall be a forced levy on all rich citizens of 1,000 millions." It was
definitely voted on September 3rd, 1793.

Single persons and widows without children were to benefit by
a basic abatement of 1,000 *livres;* married men and widows with
children by 1,500 *livres;* women to benefit by a supplementary
1,000 *livres* for each child or dependent person. The resultant lia-
bility was:

Net income livres	Loan livres
1,000	100
1,500	200
2,000	300
3,000	600
4,000	1,000
5,000	1,500
6,000	2,100
7,000	2,700
8,000	3,600
9,000	4,500
10,000	5,500
11,000	6,500

1. Girondins were the moderate party that led France in the beginning of the revolution; the Jacobins were their more radical successors.

Instalments of one-third collected in loan payments were payable in December, 1793, January, 1794, and February, 1794. *Assignats* [paper currency printed during the revolution] were cancelled and burnt, which reduced fiduciary circulation greatly. All who had not paid their share before March 1st, 1794, were, after they had been compelled to pay, deprived of all claim to subsequent repayment.

It is interesting to recall in relation to this loan that the deputy Joseph Delaunay of Angers had proposed to tax the capital of financial companies: "Let the financial companies," he proposed, "be obliged to turn over to the National Treasury, within a fortnight, a sum proportionate to their wealth. Force them to loan 20 per cent. of their capital to the Republic calculated on the current price of their shares or the rate of interest."

Revolutionary France was definitely very conscious that the counter-revolution was speculating on the financial difficulties, and aggravating them, seeking to strangle the nation. One of the reasons urged in favour of the forced loan was that it would prevent the rich from financing the counter-revolution. [Jacques-Alexis] Thuriot, member of the Convention, declared on May 20th, 1793:

> "To establish a forced loan on the rich is to obtain a great victory. These men are bound to the counter-revolution. They supply money to those in revolt in Vendée; they supply it to the emigrants; let us compel them to devote their treasures to the defence of the Republic and so make them wish for our success."

On August 24th, 1793, the Convention decreed the compilation of the Great Book of the Public Debt. It was designed to include all State creditors without distinction; the debts of the old régime, along with new debts, were all "republicanized." Holders of pre-Revolution bonds were thus given interest in the success of the Revolution. One clause permitted the conversion of 1,000 *livres* or more in *assignats* into a debt in the Great Book bearing 5 per cent. interest. Sums paid in this way were deducted from instalments due on the forced loan. In this way also the Convention sought to reduce the volume of *assignats* in circulation. On June 7th, 1793, a decree allowed a premium to purchasers of national property who fulfilled their payments in advance of the date of expiry.

Strengthening the Currency

At the same time as it attempted to reduce the circulation of *assignats*, the Convention[2] sought to increase their backing. To Church estates valued at 2,500,000,000 *livres* had been added to the property of the emigrants (nearly 2,000,000,000), the Royal forest domains (1,200,000,000) and the estates of the Order of Malta (400,000,000). In this way, a more secure backing was given to the increased currency.

But it was necessary to fight against speculation and against the manœuvres of the foreign agents. A printing press of forged *assignats*, directed by [Charles-Alexandre de] Calonne, ex-Minister of Finance of Louis XVI, operated at the headquarters of Coblenz.[3] These forged *assignats* were smuggled in to bribe collaborators and to upset the currency. The instructions given to an English spy were found:

> "Cause the exchange to rise to 200 *livres* to the pound sterling. . . . The *assignats* must be discredited as much as possible, such as do not bear the King's effigy refused. Force up the price of all commodities. If you can persuade Cott . . . to buy up tallow and candles at any price, make the public pay up to 5 *livres* per pound."

The Convention replied by severe measures against all who attempted to discredit the Republican currency. An official exchange rate of the *assignat* was finally fixed at the demand of the Commune. [William] Pitt extended special credits to enable Paris bankers to sell London stocks in Paris and so depreciate the currency and secure the transfer of capital. On July 17th, 1793, the Committee of Public Safety closed the Stock Exchange (*Bourse*); on August 1st it banned the export of capital; on August 8th it sequestrated all foreign banks.

---

2. the French government after the Republic was established   3. Coblenz was a town in Germany where Louis XVI's younger brother Louis-Stanislav-Xavier tried to organize an aristocratic counterrevolution.

Making the Rich Pay

We have just spoken of the forced loan. The great idea of Robespierre and his friends was to force the rich, whose republican integrity was suspect, to contribute to the defence of the Revolution. "When will their interest [that of the rich] blend with that of the people? Never!" wrote Robespierre in his private notebook. Moreover, in his diary he wrote: "tax the big wholesalers heavily so that the retailers can sell." The friends of Robespierre therefore carried out everywhere a policy already popular at this period which *made the rich pay.*

Robespierre condensed this policy into Article 12 of his proposed Declaration of Rights adopted on April 21st, 1793, by the Jacobins:

> "Article 12. Citizens whose income does not exceed what is necessary for their subsistence are exempted from contributing to public expenditure; others must bear it progressively to the extent of their fortune."

A few examples:

Saint-Just and Lebas, representatives on mission to Strasbourg (November, 1793) had their famous proclamation posted:

> "10,000 men are bare-footed in the Army; you must unshoe all the aristocrats of Strasbourg and to-morrow, at 10 o'clock in the morning, the 10,000 pairs of boots must be on the march to Army headquarters."

At Lyons [Jean Marie] Fouché and [Joseph] Collot d'Herbois decided that "all elderly and invalid citizens must be housed, fed, and clothed at the expense of the rich."

The representatives [Georges] Couthon and [Etienne] Maignet raised a contribution of 18,000 *livres* payable within twenty-four hours from the "egotistical rich" of Clermont: 8,000 as a dowry for four poor young girls, picked from among the families of the defenders of the nation, 7,000 in aid of the necessitous, and 3,000 to cover the expenses of a popular celebration. After Thermidor, the municipality wrote that "never had payment been made so exactly and promptly or so unjustly claimed."

Representative [Jacques Léonard] Laplanche wrote from Bourges to the Committee of Public Safety on September 29th,

1793: "My revolutionary taxes work wonders. . . . The tax that I ordered yesterday to buy means of subsistence and in part to relieve necessitous families amounted to 800,000 *livres*. You can judge as to whether I have supporters among the people and whether these revolutionary methods are of a kind to conquer all hearts for the Revolution."

Setting Maximum Prices

Finally, the last weapon of the Committee of Public Safety[4] was that of the maximum price of commodities fixed by the central power. This was imposed as a result of popular protests against the increasing prices of articles of prime necessity in consequence of speculation and monopoly.

On February 4th, 1793, the General Council of the Commune decided to prevent any increase in the price of bread by imposing a special tax of 4 millions on the rich. Two months later [Georges] Danton affirmed likewise that "it is necessary, over the whole of France, to fix the price of bread in fair proportion to the wages of the poor, any in excess will be paid by the rich." And the Convention decided: "In every Section in the Republic where the price of grain is out of fair proportion to the wages of the workers, the necessary funds raised by a levy on big fortunes will be paid by the Public Treasury to cover the excess of bread prices over the wages of necessitous citizens."

After long discussions, the principle of the maximum was established on September 29th, 1793. The Committees were charged with preparing lists of maximum prices of commodities: for produce and merchandise, they were to be based on real prices in 1790, plus one-third. A little later (October 22nd, 1793) the Convention decided to set up a Committee of Subsistence, which was to take in hand the economic government of the country. It was successively given the monopoly of imports and the right to authorize exports.

A general verdict on the effects of the maximum is difficult to give. Some seek to prove that it caused disorganization and the

4. The Committee of Public Safety was the chief executive body of the Convention (the government that established the French Republic).

disappearance of all commodities. Without denying all the difficulties encountered in its application, let us quote the opinion of a hostile observer, [Jacques] Mallet du Pan, who pointed out to the foreign Powers that with the maximum "the Convention has carried out an operation which was very economic and very popular." M.G. Lefebvre writes: "The labour of men and the value of things are subject to the fixing of prices. The maximum reduced commercial profits but left an incentive to production. Contrary to current assertions, all enterprises did not work at a loss during the Year II, but they did not realize as great profits as they might have done at the public expense of the nation. The principle was that no one had the right to gamble on the nation's peril."

Wages were fixed at the level of 1790, plus a half (instead of one-third, as for commodities); that is to say that real wages were increased nominally by one-sixth. Actually, as the workers had obtained wage increases since 1790, the maximum brought about reductions. The discontent which resulted facilitated the attack of the "corrupt" against the "Incorruptible" on Thermidor 9th, and facilitated his fall without great popular reaction.

Let us not forget that Robespierre, though in power, was never able to carry out his financial programme completely. In his speech of 8th Thermidor, he violently attacked [Pierre Joseph] Cambon: "The counter-revolution has control of our finances." He accused him of "favouring rich creditors, of ruining poor men, and of bringing them to despair, thus increasing discontent." Cambon, always an adversary of Robespierre, was after Thermidor[5] considered too revolutionary. He was to know both prison and exile. . . .

Jacobins' Economic Success

We have attempted to bring out the fundamental tendencies of the Revolution in the realm of finance. But how many comparisons force themselves, even when care is taken not to envisage the past in terms of present-day circumstances, but to see the facts in relation to the historic events which accompanied and determined them!

5. the new leaders after the Jacobins were overthrown

If, in [Jean] Jaurès' formula, we seek in the French Revolution the solution of all our present political problems, we see that in finance, at any rate, the Revolution—the Jacobins—proved that democracy restores finances, while the big bourgeoisie throws them into disorder and leads the way to bankruptcy. This study has shown that methods adopted by the Jacobins—making the rich pay, banning the export of capital, controlling the banks—enabled them to secure the independence of the French Republic against the men of Coblenz and their foreign allies. When our Communist Party repeats after Robespierre, after Jules Guesde, "Suppression of indirect taxation. Progressive tax on incomes," when it demands a levy on big fortunes, the nationalization of monopolies, and the control of banks, it preserves the true tradition of the French revolutionaries. In Lenin's words, "it aims at all that the eighteenth century Jacobins achieved that was great, indestructible, and unforgettable."

Viewpoint 3

"[During the revolution] women of the middle and lower classes acquired new outlooks about themselves and their role in society."

French Women Attained Lasting Political Power During the French Revolution

Darline Gay Levy, Harriet Branson Applewhite, and Mary Durham Johnson

In the following excerpt from their book, *Women in Revolutionary Paris: 1789–1795*, Darline Gay Levy, Harriet Branson Applewhite, and Mary Durham Johnson contend that French revolutionary women were able to make a lasting political impact on their country. Although Levy, Applewhite, and Johnson acknowledge that many of the political gains women made in the early years of the French Revolution had eroded by 1795, the authors argue that women in later decades were inspired by those early efforts, helping them effect lasting change in French society.

171

The authors assert that France's revolutionary women became "barometers of political crises," whose demands could not be neglected. They also maintain that French women contributed to the political education of children. Levy is a history professor at New York University, Applewhite is a political science professor at Southern Connecticut State University in New Haven, and Johnson has taught at Temple University in Philadelphia and East Tennessee State University in Johnson City.

A fter June, 1795, it seemed that the women of Paris were a failure as a political force. First of all, they had lost their supporting institutions. Their clubs were closed, they were shut out of the galleries of the Convention, popular societies were disbanded, and workshops were closed. After that there was no longer any way to coordinate the political efforts of women of all social ranks. Furthermore, once the Jacobins [a radical revolutionary party] had co-opted populist principles and programs, the radical left disintegrated. Finally, the repressive tactics of the Thermidorians [the group that overthrew the Jacobins] were effective. In the aftermath of the Prairial Days[1] a special Military Tribunal and Section committees ordered the arrest and imprisonment of the most articulate and dedicated male and female leaders among the common people. Police had become adept at unearthing clandestine organizations, spying, infiltrating bread lines and marketplaces. While such tactics also dissolved the political power of the male *sans-culottes*[2] and prevented the mutual support between men and women that had been effective in the Year II [September 1793 to September 1794], one could also assert that the male revolutionary leadership deliberately reduced women to a narrow but exalted role—that of bearing, nurturing, and educating future citizens.

Successive governments under the Directory and [French leader]

1. On 1–4 Prairial, Year III (May 20–23, 1795), a largely female group surrounded the Convention Hall in Paris and tried to force the legislature to implement a democratic constitution.   2. *Sans-culottes* ("without breeches") were politically radical workers known for wearing long trousers in opposition to the breeches worn by aristocrats.

Napoleon [Bonaparte] made deliberate efforts to prevent crowds from congregating and women from having any impact on public affairs. Even the legal and civic gains women had made in the first six years of the Revolution were eroded after 1795. During the Directory, laws pertaining to the establishment of primary schools for girls were poorly enforced, and *citoyenne* became an exclusive title for respectable ladies and female friends of the national representatives. The Napoleonic Code did not perpetuate most of the revolutionary advances in women's legal equality, such as in property administration and child custody. The Code did keep equal inheritance and did permit divorce, until the Restoration [of the monarchy]. In general, married women were considered legal minors and were denied ownership of property. Moreover, married women were forbidden to make contracts without their father's or husband's consent, and the double standard of morality was incorporated in private law dealing with divorce, child custody, and alimony. The Napoleonic Code rendered the position of French women less advantageous than it had been in the Old Regime. Before the Revolution, women of the religious and lay aristocracy had been able to handle property and legal matters which pertained to their estates and families; the Napoleonic Code treated *all* women equally and prevented those of high social status from exerting any power in public and familial matters.

Women's Political Contributions

But the involvement of the women of Paris in the Revolution did have a lasting impact on French politics and society in spite of the numerous setbacks to women in the aftermath of Year II. Furthermore, women of the middle and lower classes acquired new outlooks about themselves and their role in society which could not be erased by patriarchal attitudes and laws.

First, women in the Revolution accentuated their impact on government officials in times of crisis. In fact, the involvement of large numbers of women in protest was taken by both national and local authorities as a signal of the seriousness of the breakdown of control. When scarcity and prices made women desperate, there was no way to control the streets. Furthermore, after the Revolution any war policy had to accommodate the particular needs of women: pensions for widows or wives of disabled soldiers, adequate uniforms and provisions for husbands and sons in the army, workshops for women, and so on. If such demands were neglected, women would be sure to come threatening and shouting into the galleries of national legislatures and local assemblies. Thus, the Revolution carried forward and intensified the roles of women as barometers of political crises and as potent threats of a breakdown in control of the city. The Revolution did not create these roles for women, but it magnified the national political repercussions of their protest.

A second legacy of revolutionary women is their contribution to political education. Women had become conscious of their roles as makers of patriots and had come to put a high value on education in general and education for politics in particular.

Changes in Family Life

There are a number of . . . profound ways in which the Revolution benefited women in a lasting way.

For example, comparing the evolution of demographic statistics with the dates of political events produces some surprising and significant results. . . . Let us . . . look at marriages. After all the vast majority of women expected and sought marriage as a normal completion of their lives. In 1966 Marcel Reinhard, a French historian who had a special interest in this field of studies, contributed an essay which summed up the demographic impact of the Revolution in two apparently contradictory conclusions.

The first:

> The most striking trend is the marked increase in the marriage rate. Comparing the annual mean with that of the two decades preceding and following 1789 the increase is often from twenty to twenty-five per cent, sometimes fifty and even sixty per cent or more, both in the rural areas and the towns. . . . To sum up, the major effect of the Rev-

Women who were political oddities, like Olympe de Gouges or Etta Palm d'Aelders, may not have originated a feminist movement, but they did help to legitimate the idea that women had something to say about politics that could not be discounted or laughed off by those in power. Women were influential as the main transmitters of political values to their children, especially attitudes toward authority and toward political participation.

The content of French political vocabulary and myth was permanently transformed by women in revolutionary Paris. Political style is an important element of any political culture because it determines the ways in which the content of politics will be felt, transmitted, and understood. French political style is both highly verbal and highly visual. Modern French political analysts have often commented on the persistence of revolutionary rhetoric in

---

olution was the increase in the number of marriages.

But only a couple of pages later, in his general conclusion, Reinhard contradicts himself in a rather startling fashion: 'The major demographic effect of the Revolution is certainly the accentuation of the tendency to limit births. This is an extraordinary factor' Reinhard continues, 'as an increase in fecundity is evident in Belgium and England at the same time.'

Let us forget the quibble about which was the *really* major demographic effect. We are still left with two of them.

The French Revolution coincided with a significant turning point in the experience of Frenchwomen: the marriage rate went up and the birth rate went down. Looking a bit further ahead we find these changes still operating strongly during the first years of the nineteenth century, for Louis Bergeron, the historian of the Napoleonic Empire tells us that while the marriage rate continued higher than before 1789, and while the population had grown by several millions, there were about ten per cent fewer births between 1811 and 1815 than between 1781 and 1784.

Barrie Rose, *Australian Journal of Politics and History*, 1994.

the twentieth century. Much of this symbolism is associated with women: their knitting needles, their wooden shoes stamping approval or outrage in the galleries of the National Convention or the Jacobin Society, the tricolored ribbons in their bonnets, the pikes in their hands. As we have seen in the documents, these symbols were meaningful within the context of revolutionary politics and remain in the political culture as evocative symbols of approval, disapproval, or disgust.

To the 1848 generation of Parisian revolutionary women, the women of the eighteenth-century Revolution were important for more than their symbolic inspiration. The Society of Revolutionary Republican Women became the prototype of political clubs for women that flourished in 1848. The two presidents [Claire] Lacombe and [Pauline] Léon, were extolled for their attacks on the bourgeoisie and their championship of the interests of working women. . . .

A Revolutionary Legacy

Prerevolutionary political nationalization was carried forward by the revolutionary leadership and most fully by the Jacobins, with a significant innovation in the form of institutions for mass political participation. The national legislatures, the Commune, the National Guard, the Section assemblies, the societies, the clubs, and so on, brought people together to act on their needs and demands. Some of the women of Paris demanded and acted upon their rights to full political participation in these institutions. Women were not mere tools of male agitators and radical journalists, as so many conservative historians and writers have argued. It is clear in the documents that men and women had differing perceptions and expectations of women in the new society. Male revolutionaries had granted women the honorary title of *citoyennes* without expecting that women would want to try to exercise full rights of political autonomy. But the women took their title seriously.

Sometimes the women demanded literal equality in modern political power: the right to bear arms, the vote, a national assembly of women. They were most effective, however, when they made their traditional demands for subsistence and economic security.

On these issues they were able to forge an alliance with the radical left in Parisian politics, culminating in their closeness to the Enragés[3] in 1793. These issues were their traditional economic grievances, but it is our contention that these issues became a bridge to modern political activities. In the early months of the Revolution, demands for bread and subsistence were presented through symbolic acting out, as if the women were in rehearsal trying out new roles. In their marches early in the fall of 1789, and when they played legislators for a day at Versailles in October, they were emerging as autonomous political actors.

As the Revolution unfolded, such behavior became institutionalized in galleries, clubs, and popular societies. Once the Revolutionary Government had consolidated power, it did not or could not share authority with the new structures of political democracy while fighting a simultaneous international and civil war and combatting subversion. Ultimately, of course, the people were empowered only as plebiscitory supporters of a dictator. Thus, fully egalitarian democracy was ephemeral in French politics for the women as well as the men. But it set a precedent. The lessons in civic behavior and exposure to public affairs were not forgotten. In the events of 1848 and 1871 women revived the spirit of the Parisian women of 1789 and 1793, although they learned to correct mistakes made by their predecessors in tactics, organization, and relations with male revolutionaries. They remembered that their eighteenth-century revolutionary forebears were becoming citizens with an articulate voice in their neighborhoods, their city, and their nation. The women of revolutionary Paris take their places in history as integral parts of the revolutionary legacy to the future; their influence was not to last, but it was not to be forgotten.

3. Enragés were a small group of Parisian radical extremists who campaigned for strict economic controls.

Viewpoint 4

"The Napoleonic codes swept away almost every advance [French] women had made."

French Women Did Not Attain Lasting Political Power During the French Revolution

Jane Abray

French women were thwarted in their attempts to improve their political standing during the revolutionary era, Jane Abray contends in the following viewpoint. In Abray's opinion, this failure was caused by the lack of support from the revolutionary governments and the inability of French feminists to expand their narrow base. Abray explains that although women were granted more freedom in private affairs—such as inheritance, property rights, and divorce—legislators outlawed women's political clubs. Eventually, even the advances in civil law that benefited women were swept away when Napoleon took control of the nation. In addition, Abray maintains that French feminists failed to work with each other and were not able to change the

Jane Abray, "Feminism in the French Revolution," *The American Historical Review*, vol. 80, February 1975, pp. 43–62. Copyright © 1975 by American Historical Association. Reproduced by permission of the publisher and the author.

opinions of most French women, who generally accepted traditional definitions of gender roles. Abray concludes that the failure of revolutionary feminism shows how the French Revolution was, despite its political upheaval, an essentially
conservative era. Abray is a professor of history at the University
of Toronto.

French feminism has a long history; its roots go back far beyond
the tumult of new ideas that mark the Revolution. Since the
Renaissance, indeed since the Middle Ages, French women—and
men—had argued for equality of legal and political rights for the
sexes. Woman's education, her economic position, and her relationship to her father and husband had all been worked over time
after time. In the eighteenth century intellectuals carried on a
desultory debate over the status of women. The discussion slowly
grew more heated until, in the early years of the Revolution, a
small group of bold thinkers demanded changes that, if effected,
would have altered the character of French civilization far more
than did the abolition of the monarchy.

Single or married, women had few rights in the law during the
last decades of the *ancien régime* [France's pre-Revolution gov-
ernment]. Their testimony could be accepted in criminal and civil
courts but not for notarized acts like wills. In some parts of France
a single woman could enter into contractual relationships, but for
the most part her rights—reasonably extensive as late as the thirteenth century—had atrophied. . . .

Female Citizenship

Under the Old Regime women could sometimes vote and act as re-
gents; during the Revolution they assumed their right to form political associations. Less than five years after the calling of the
Estates-General[1] this had all disappeared. The legislators barely considered female suffrage despite the heated arguments the feminists

1. The Estates-General was the pre-Revolutionary political body that represented
Frances's three estates, or classes.

had put forward. Abbé Emmanuel-Joseph Sieyès voiced the general opinion as early as July 1789. 'Women, at least as things now stand, children, foreigners, in short those who contribute nothing to the public establishment, should have no direct influence on the government.' The systematization of French electoral law eliminated the idiosyncrasies that had permitted women to vote; for the first time in centuries women were completely barred, as a group, from this aspect of the political process. Few people protested this exclusion. The women of Droits de l'Homme [section] in Paris and the Républicaines Révolutionnaires castigated the provisions of the Constitution of 1793, but only by making speeches in the latter's club. Possibly the infrequency with which elections were held took the sting out of this exclusion; certainly at the level where politics really mattered, in the clubs and sections, women continued to vote for a time. Probably exclusion from the regency also mattered little, particularly when everyone was soon excluded by the abolition of the monarchy. The regency was not an important issue in itself, but it shows the ease with which the legislators could dismiss the idea of women participating in government.

Far more important to ordinary women than the vote or the regency was the issue of citizenship. Were women citizens enough to take the civic oath, one of the central means of demonstrating acceptance of the revolutionary ideals and of participating in communal life? In 1790, when the National Assembly[2] swore the oath, the spectators, men and women, joined them. Within two months women's right to take the oath had become an issue. Brigent Baudouin, wife of a municipal officer in Lanion, wrote the Assembly on behalf of several women in her village. 'There is not a word about women in the Constitution, and I admit that they can take no part in government; nevertheless mothers can and should be citizens.' They should therefore, she continued, be permitted to swear the revolutionary oath before the municipal officers. Goupil de Préfeln, a member of the Cercle Social, moved that all married women of 'respectable conduct' be granted this honor. He added that mothers undoubtedly had more right to it than did childless

2. The National Assembly was the name adopted by the Estates-General during the early stages of the Revolution.

women. The motion was tabled. Swearing civic oaths became particularly important in the summer of 1790 during the Fêtes de la Fédération. In Beaune the National Guard invited eighty-four women to the ceremony, but the municipal authorities firmly refused to let them take part. In Toulouse the city officials, momentarily forgetting *la galanterie française* [French gallantry], turned the fire hoses on the women present to disperse them. Examples could be found of women who did take the oath and who were invited to sign petitions and make other symbolic gestures— for example, at the Champs de Mars in 1791—but the whole issue of women's citizenship remained clouded. With no sure rule to which to appeal, women had to depend on the good will of local authorities. Even at this low, but symbolically vital, level women's political status continued to be a matter of privileges not rights. The Committee of Public Safety and the Directory would both find themselves dealing with the consequences. A representative on mission, J. -B. Jérôme Bô, wrote the committee in 1794 to advise exemplary punishment of troublemakers, especially of those women who claimed that the law could not touch them because they had not taken the civic oath. In 1796 some factions used women to create disorder; since the government did not take them seriously, women could get away with subversive speeches for which men could be jailed.

The revolutionary governments had at one time taken women's activities quite seriously, but only long enough to outlaw their clubs. Apparently article 7 of the second Declaration of Rights, guaranteeing the rights of free speech and assembly, no more applied to women than did article 5, which promised equal access to public office for all citizens. The Mountain [consisting of Maximillien Robespierre, Georges-Jacques Danton, and Jean-Paul Marati] sent the women's clubs crashing down in the fall of 1793. The ostensible cause was the unrevolutionary conduct of the Républicaines Révolutionnaires, a charge that could be supported in fact by the admiration of Claire Lacombe and Pauline Léon for Jacques Roux, Théophile Leclerc, and the *enragés*.[3] The campaign

---

3. *Enragés* were a small group of Parisian radical extremists who campaigned for strict economic controls.

against the Républicaines began in the Jacobin club[4] on a strictly political note. A member announced that the women had taken up with Leclerc; François Chabot, Claude Basire, and Taschereau spoke against Lacombe's new political line. 'I do not doubt that she is a tool of the counterrevolution,' said Chabot sagely. At this point the campaign against the Républicaines was specifically political and focused on them alone. Yet how soon the campaign changed! A month later a deputation of women from several sections came to the Convention to protest the activities of the Républicaines; one of them requested the abolition of their club. The Convention forwarded their complaint to the Committee of General Security. Fabre d'Eglantine made good use of this opportunity to address the Convention. After the *bonnet rouge* [red cap], which the Républicaines wore during their meetings, comes the gun belt, then the gun, he warned. He reminded the Convention of the manner in which the women went after bread: like pigs at a trough. These were not good mothers and daughters but— significant although false characterization—'des filles émancipées, des grenadiers femelles' ["emancipated women, female grenade throwers"]. The members several times interrupted his speech with applause. A little later one of the women spectators came forward to demand the abolition of all women's clubs.

The Convention must have been gratified by the report André Amar soon presented on behalf of the Committee of General Security. That committee, explained Amar, had considered two questions: should women exercise political rights and take part in government, and should women meet in political associations? From the specific case of the Républicaines Révolutionnaires the government had moved to consider the status of all French women. To both questions the committee replied in the negative. Women did not have the strength of character needed to govern; political meetings took them away from 'the more important concerns to which nature calls them.' Nature's imperious commands were not to be violated; women could have no political rights. Amar concluded:

> There is another aspect of women's associations that seems dangerous. If we take into account the fact that the political education of men is still at its very beginnings, that all the

principles are not yet developed, and that we still stammer over the word 'liberty,' then how much less enlightened are women, whose moral education has been practically nonexistent. Their presence in the *sociétés populaires* [popular societies], then, would give an active part in government to persons exposed to error and seduction even more than are men. And, let us add that women, by their constitution, are open to an exaltation which could be ominous in public life. The interests of the state would soon be sacrificed to all the kinds of disruption and disorder that hysteria can produce. . . .

Further Feminist Failures

The suppression of the women's clubs effectively destroyed the feminists' political aspirations. It was not, however, the clearest statement on women's rights the government made. After the *journée of Iᵉʳ* Prairial of the Year III (May 20, 1795) [September 1794 to September 1795][4] the Convention voted to exclude women from its meetings; in future they would be allowed to watch only if they were accompanied by a man carrying a citizen's card. Three days later the Convention placed all Parisian women under a kind of house arrest. 'All women are to return to their domiciles until otherwise ordered. Those found on the streets in groups of more than five one hour after the posting of this order will be dispersed by force and then held under arrest until public tranquillity is restored in Paris.' The progress of the Revolution had rendered the brave hopes of the feminists of 1789–91 chimeric.

Only in regard to their legal status could feminists find some gratification. The Revolution, so severe to women in public life, was kinder to them in private life. Inheritance laws were changed to guarantee male and female children equal rights. Women reached majority at twenty-one under the new laws. Moreover they could contract debts and be witnesses in civil acts. Other legislation changed the laws concerning women's property, giving

4. On 1–4 Prairial, Year III (May 20–23, 1795), a largely female group surrounded the Convention Hall in Paris and tried to force the legislature to implement a democratic constitution.

them some voice in its administration, and acknowledged the mother's part in decisions affecting her children. Revolutionary divorce legislation treated both sexes equally. Yet some inequalities remained. Women could not serve on juries; in practice they were excluded from sitting on the Tribunaux de Famille, which attempted to settle family quarrels from 1790 to 1796. Moreover the gains were short-lived. The Napoleonic codes swept away almost every advance the women had made, returning them to the status [Robert Joseph] Pothier had described in 1769 [one of complete dependence].

The most important reason for the almost total failure of revolutionary feminism was its narrow base. Feminism was and remained a minority interest. The majority of French women—the logical constituency to which the movement could hope to appeal—had no interest in changing their social position. For the most part French women accepted the eighteenth-century definition of femininity. Far more typical of their attitudes than any of the feminist manifestoes is this speech made by the women of Épinal to their men.

> If our strength had equaled our courage we would, like you, have hastened to take up weapons and would have shared with you the glory of having won our freedom. But it took stronger arms than ours to defeat the enemies of the Constitution; our weakness has prevented us from taking part in this Revolution. We content ourselves with admiring your efforts.

The feminist movement had been unable to reach these women. Neither its words nor its action had made any sense to ordinary women. Feminism never became part of the programme of the majority of the women's clubs. Only the Besançon club considered urging the Convention to extend the suffrage to women, but faced with the mockery of local Jacobins it soon abandoned its project. At Orléans feminism never raised its head. One of the few lengthy series of *procès-verbaux* available from a women's club, that of Ruffec (Charente), shows not a hint of feminist attitudes in two years. The women's clubs were content to function as auxiliaries to male societies. The mixed clubs held themselves equally aloof, except for the short-lived efforts of the Cercle Social. If the various *sociétés fraternelles des deux sexes* [fraternal societies of the two sexes] approved of feminism, they kept the secret to themselves. . . .

Feminist Errors

The feminists made tactical and strategic errors. Women's groups allowed themselves to be distracted too easily. The Républicaines Révolutionnaires let themselves become embroiled in street fights over the wearing of the *cocarde* [cockade] and the *bonnet rouge*. All of the women's clubs suffered from their habit of putting other people's causes before their own. The provincial clubs settled meekly into ladies' aid societies, and even the fiery Républicaines were more interested in the price of bread than in women's wages. However commendable these positions may have been as expressions of largeness of spirit, they were sorely damaging to any attempt to work specific, radical change. The feminists showed other signs of political and managerial inexperience. They acted in isolation: individual leaders had no verifiable contacts with each other; the clubs proceeded independently, and the occasional attempts to set up a national organization came to nothing.

It would seem, too, that that vague entity, the spirit of the times, ran counter to the feminist revolution. One important aspect of this counter-current was the ideal of the nuclear family. Time and again feminists tripped over the conviction that the changes they advocated were unnatural because women belonged in the home. This was the most frequent explanation given for refusing their requests. The idea of the family as a secure nest, maintained by the wife, to which the husband retired from his toil in the outside world, was a relatively recent development. It certainly did not reflect the reality of lower-class life, for lower-class women could not afford to spend all their time keeping house. It was the wealthy who developed a hagiographic tradition around the family. Once women were firmly confined to the home there was no 'need' for feminism, and the majority of middle-class politicians could only gaze upon it in blank astonishment. To their way of thinking, refusing the feminists' demands ought to have been counted as so many acts of kindness toward women, who were by nature too delicate for the dirty world into which the feminists tried to thrust them.

Revolutionary feminism began in a burst of enthusiasm. Its unpopularity, its own mistakes, and the blissful incomprehension and dogmatism of its opponents combined to obliterate it. While it lasted it was a very real phenomenon with a comprehensive programme for social change, perhaps the most far-reaching such programme of the Revolution. This very radicalism ensured that it would remain a minority movement, almost the preserve of crackpots. Influential contemporaries turned out speech after speech, newspaper after newspaper, report after report without ever acknowledging its existence. Despite its minority nature and its abject failure, revolutionary feminism is not without significance. It illustrates, as clearly as anything can, the changing seasons of the Revolutionary calendar and stands as striking proof of the essential social conservatism of this political upheaval.

Viewpoint 5

"The French Revolution accelerated the growth of nationalism, secularized it and thereby helped to set it above all other values."

The French Revolution Spurred a Greater Respect for the Nation-State

Conor Cruise O'Brien

Prior to the mid-nineteenth century, several European nations, most notably Germany and Italy, were a loose group of kingdoms and territories that were not wholly unified. In the following viewpoint Conor Cruise O'Brien asserts that the French Revolution helped accelerate the growth of nationalism throughout nineteenth- and twentieth-century Europe, particularly in Germany. He acknowledges that nationalism existed prior to, and helped cause, the revolution, but argues that the French Revolution helped elevate love of the nation-state to a powerful political force. According to O'Brien, Germany experienced this intense love for a country and its native people most strongly. Unfortunately, however, German nationalism soon became imbued with racist and anti-Semitic attitudes, he contends. O'Brien is a politician, journalist, and historian who has written more than twenty books.

Within ten years of the beginning of the Revolution, revolutionary internationalism seemed to have turned to ashes. The French Revolution had made a mockery of *les républiques soeurs* [sister republics] and had insisted that *patriotes* be puppets. What stood out, in contrast with those international shams, was the huge exalted and long-triumphant national reality: *la grande nation* itself. It is hardly surprising if succeeding generations were less inclined to emulate what now looked like shams than to emulate a triumphant reality, with the glory that it seemed to trail.

The expansion of French political hegemony under the Revolution and the Empire did much to destroy France's former *cultural* hegemony. The symbolic figure in that respect may appear as Count Rostopchin, Governor of Moscow, starting to learn *Russian* in 1812, while the French armies were approaching his city. He and his kind were being taught by the French themselves that they were Russians and must learn 'their own language'. The international culture of Europe's Francophone aristocracy was breaking down, more or less as the international religious system of the Counter-Reformation had broken down, and as the effort to create revolutionary and post-revolutionary international systems around the French example had broken down. Multiple forms of nationalism were to be the main heirs of the failed internationals. New forms of *inter*nationalism were to be attempted also, by Marx and others in the later nineteenth century, and to be replaced in their turn, in the twentieth century, by new nationalist entities in international dress: Soviet Union, China, Vietnam, Cambodia, Yugoslavia, Romania, Albania etc., all theoretically part of 'international communism'.

The Relationship Between Nationalism and Revolution

Nationalism should not be—as it sometimes is—seen as 'caused' by the French Revolution. Rather, . . . the growth of nationalism is among the causes of the French Revolution and of its expansion. And a part of what we see as 'reactions to the French Revolution' is rooted in reaction against French international cultural hegemony *before* the French Revolution. 'Spit out that green slime of the Seine'—meaning the French language—cried [Johann Gottfried von] Herder in Germany in the 1770s; two generations before Rostopchin, in beleaguered Moscow, brought himself to spit it out.

The most that can be said is that the French Revolution accelerated the growth of nationalism, secularized it and thereby helped to set it above all other values. That tendency seems to have been at work, in different and sometimes contradictory ways, from Waterloo [the site of Napoleon's final defeat] on, throughout the nineteenth and into the twentieth century.

Nationalism—the nationalisms of the English, the Russians, the Prussians and the Spaniards—was probably the main force that defeated Napoleon; just as French nationalism was the main force that sustained him. But the victorious powers—meaning the ruling classes of post-Waterloo Europe—were in general highly suspicious of nationalism. They disliked enthusiasm of all kinds, and nationalism is one of the most disquieting forms of enthusiasm. Some of the victors—the Austrian and Russian Empires in particular—had practical reasons to fear the rise of nationalism among their subject peoples. In general, the restored dynasts and aristocrats suspected both liberalism and nationalism as twin manifestations of a possibly renascent Jacobinism [referring to the revolutionary Jacobin party]: bourgeois power. And all of them were watchful for warning signs of a revival of the most alarming of all possible forms of nationalism: that of the now suppressed *grande nation* itself.

France and Germany in the Nineteenth Century

The main focus of resurgent nationalism in nineteenth-century Europe was the Franco-German interaction. The crucial year was 1848. This was, of course, a year of multiple, national revolutions, mostly unsuccessful, led by bourgeois, with some backing from workers and peasants, and conducted under both liberal and nationalist slogans, with a nostalgic symbolism of French Revolutionary type (tricolours etc.).

The seminal events of that year, the events that were to shape the course of modern history, occurred in Paris and in Frankfurt.

The events of Paris were relatively simple and appeared—at least at first—as the major success of the Year of Revolutions. The cautious and uncharismatic House of Orleans fell, never to return. What replaced it, after a short interval, was Louis-Napoleon Bonaparte, first as Prince-President, and then as Napoleon III, Emperor of the French. Europe was put under notice that *la grande nation*, under the inherited name of its most illustrious champion, was once more in quest of *la gloire:* other nationalisms were stimulated, as before.

What happened in Frankfurt was more complex, and also more ominous. The Frankfurt Parliament offered the Imperial Crown of Germany to the King of Prussia, Friedrich Wilhelm IV, who refused to accept the Crown, from the Parliament. The offer signalized the desire of German nationalists, including liberals, to place themselves under the leadership of Prussia. The refusal of that particular offer, at that particular time, signified that if German unity was to be achieved it would have to be on Prussia's terms, and at Prussia's chosen time.

Prussia's relation to German nationalism had been ambiguous. It was from the Prussian capital that [German philosopher Johann Gottlieb] Fichte's seminal *Addresses to the German Nation* had gone forth. And it was to Prussia that German nationalists necessarily looked for leadership. It was Prussia, alone in Germany, that had played a heroic role against Napoleon, and had helped to bring about his downfall, through the battles of Leipzig and Waterloo. So Prussia was the Germanic heir of the Napoleonic charisma. But the Hohenzollerns [Germany's most politically powerful family] distrusted the noisy nationalism of the *Burschenschaften* and *Turnvereine* (gymnastic societies and students' associations). That was South-German stuff, bourgeois, civilian, tainted with neo-Jacobin hankerings after liberalism and democracy. The nationalists might be useful, in opening the imperial way for Prussia, but they would have to dance to Prussia's tune, not Prussia to theirs. And that tune would have nothing in common with the *Marseillaise.*

Ironically, the Hohenzollern attitude towards German nationalists outside Prussia paralleled that of [Maximilien] Robespierre towards foreign *patriotes*. And this is logical enough. For was not Prussia the core of the *new* Grand Nation?

Changes After 1870

1870 marks—along with much else—a change in the meaning and associations of nationalism. With the debacle of the last Bonaparte, the French and revolutionary aspects of the nationalist heritage became devalued; the *counter*-revolutionary aspects, long present, are enhanced. With the triumph of Prussianized Germany, nationalism takes on an increasingly Germanic tone, not only in Germany itself, but on *both* sides of the Rhine, and consequently throughout Europe. Nationalism becomes more and more an affair of the right, and more and more charged with racism. The French revolutionary heritage, now understood in an *inter*nationalist sense, becomes the heritage of the left, almost exclusively.

Nationalism in Imperial Germany was right-wing *ex-officio:* supreme authority always remained in the hands of an aristocratic military elite, which German nationalists supported to the bitter end. The only aspect of the French revolutionary tradition which Imperial Germany made its own to a significant extent was glorification and quasi-divinization of the state ([Georg] Rousseau-[Abbé] Sieyès, Germanized through [Jean Jacques] Hegel). But it was a somewhat watered down, semi-Christianized version. The state itself was not the supreme value; it was only the walk of God on earth: *Der Gang Gottes an der Erde.* In all other respects, the nationalism of Imperial Germany is in sharp contrast to French revolutionary nationalism. But German nationalism—even before the triumph of the Prussian elite—was also distinct from the French revolutionary kind in another important aspect (besides the aristocratic one). This was the special German emphasis on the purity of the *Volk* [German people]: an emphasis which, after 1870, became more and more explicitly racist.

The theory was that the German *Volk*, never having been conquered by the Romans, remained pure, both linguistically and racially, unlike the French and the English. This theory is already present in the 1770s in Herder, though mildly expressed as is usually his way. After the Napoleonic impact, *Völkisch* nationalism became strident in Fichte and his following. This was quite congenial to the authorities of the new Germany, after 1870. The idea of a hereditary elite is itself a racist idea, so that the rising influence of racism within German nationalism bolstered the authority of Germany's Prussian ruling class.

In France, the collapse and disintegration of Bonapartism after Sedan [where Napoleon III was captured in 1870] led to the emergence of a right-wing nationalism, rejecting not merely Bonapartism but the entire heritage both of the French Revolution and of the Enlightenment itself. French nationalism, while virulently Germanophobe in form and intent, in fact imitated its victorious adversary. The compliment which German nationalism had paid to the French kind, after Jena [site of a Napoleon I victory in 1806], was returned by the French nationalists, after Sedan.

The German cult of the purity of the *Volk*—a cult which persists today among the Afrikaner *volk*—took root, to a more limited but still significant extent, among the French right also. Antisemitism became the most conspicuous common feature of the nationalist right on both sides of the Rhine. And the fact that antisemitism was now *à la mode* in the most civilized countries of the Continent probably helped the rulers of Russia to return to old-fashioned persecuting anti-semitism from 1881 on. Among the Jews themselves, those who were most clearly conscious of the way the wind was blowing were the Zionists. The rediscovery of Jewish nationalism, in the late nineteenth century, was a response to the discovery that the European nationalisms had turned racist.

Destructive Nationalism

Nationalism had been a force in pre-revolutionary France, and had played its part, along with Enlightenment, in the pre-revolutionary process. Nationalism had become dominant in the Revolution itself, in the expansion of the Revolution, and in the Empire of the Emperor of the French. French revolutionary universalism had been mainly a matter of rhetoric, and the cynicism of its manipulators had led to the bitter disillusionment of the international sympathizers. Yet through the authority of the rhetoric, some of the Enlightenment tradition was preserved and transmitted within nationalism up to 1870 (and thereafter also, to some extent, on the margins of Europe). Though there are traces of racism in some Enlightenment writers—Voltaire's anti-semitic gibes, for example—the Enlightenment tradition as a whole, being both tolerant and universalist, worked against active racism. It was only after nationalism, under German leadership, had liberated itself from almost all French revolutionary influence, and then from the whole Enlightenment, that mainstream nationalism turned racist and anti-semitic.

In the triumphal period of Wilhelmine Germany, the racism of German nationalism remained largely intellectual and social. But defeat in the First World War activated the manically destructive forces latent in the new nationalism. The only major common feature between the nationalism of the French Revolution and the nationalism of the National Socialists was the concept of the nation-state as the supreme value. In that respect, the National Socialists were closer to the French Revolutionaries than they were to Wilhelmine Germany, since the Nazis, like the French Revolutionaries, were radically deChristianized, and so able to go the full length, in deifying the nation-state. But the nature of the nation-state so deified had radically changed, through the introduction of the Germanic concept of the need to defend the purity of the *Volk*. The deification of a racist nation-state, biologically inimical to certain other races, produced a modern Moloch,[1] and the Holocaust.

1. the Canaanite god of fire, to whom children were sacrificed

Viewpoint 6

"The discussion of rights developed during the French Revolution."

The French Revolution Produced a Greater Respect for the Individual

Lynn Hunt

Prior to the French Revolution, most of France's inhabitants lacked basic human rights such as political representation and economic freedom; power was held largely in the hands of the king, aristocracy, and clergy. The French Revolution is important because it helped establish the idea of human rights, Lynn Hunt asserts in the following viewpoint. Hunt explains that French legislators were influenced by British and American documents, including the 1689 English Bill of Rights and Thomas Jefferson's Declaration of Independence. According to Hunt, the French belief in individual rights culminated in the Declaration of the Rights of Man and Citizen, adopted in August 1789, which gave French citizens the right to free speech, a free press, and equality under the law. She further notes that the discussion of human rights continued in France during the revolutionary era, al-

Lynn Hunt, *The French Revolution and Human Rights: A Brief Documentary History*. Boston, MA: Bedford Books, 1996. Copyright © 1996 by Bedford Books/St. Martin's Press, Inc. Reproduced by permission.

though some rights were suppressed during the violent regime known as the Terror. Despite these setbacks, Hunt concludes, the idea of human rights originally expressed by the French during the revolution eventually progressed throughout Europe and the rest of the world. Hunt is the Eugen Weber Professor of modern European history at the University of California at Los Angeles and the author or editor of several volumes on the French Revolution, including *The French Revolution and Human Rights: A Brief Documentary History*, the source of the following viewpoint.

The idea of universal human rights *is* Western in origin. It did not appear all at once but slowly emerged in the eighteenth century, in large part as a reaction to contemporary political conflicts—in Great Britain, between Great Britain and its North American colonies, and in France. Its sources varied from new conceptions of individual autonomy (the belief that individuals should make their own decisions about marriage, for example) to debates about the foundations of government. What is most distinctive about Western notions of human rights is the emphasis on their universal applicability; by implication, human rights are for all humans, not just for one nation or group. . . .

American and English Influences

The American War of Independence had helped make notions of human rights even more influential in France, for many of the French officers who served in North America arrived home fired by the ideals of liberty that they saw in action in the New World. Thomas Jefferson's Declaration of Independence of 1776 put the Enlightenment position on rights into a declarative, political form: "We hold these truths to be self-evident: that all men are created equal; that they are endowed by their Creator with certain inalienable rights; that among these are life, liberty and the pursuit of happiness"—happiness being an Enlightenment addition to [John] Locke's original list of rights. The protection of these rights justified colonial resistance to Great Britain, but this was as far as the declaration went; it had no legal relationship to the constitutions written later.

When declaring their rights the Americans drew on the constitutional tradition that they had inherited from the English. English Parliaments regularly cited King John's Great Charter of English liberties, the Magna Carta of 1215. The constitutional conflicts between the English Crown and Parliament in the seventeenth century inspired a renewal of the declaratory urge, as Parliament forced Charles I to accept a Petition of Right in 1628[1] and then insisted that the newly crowned William and Mary agree to a Bill of Rights in 1689. These documents reaffirmed the "ancient rights and liberties" of Englishmen as represented in English common law and the customary relations between Crown and Parliament; they grew out of English legal traditions and constitutional quarrels rather than a universal human rights philosophy. Locke's writings, forged in the midst of these very English struggles, helped turn the idea of rights and liberties in a more universalistic direction. . . .

However much the subject of political negotiation and compromise at the time, [the Declaration of the Rights of Man and Citizen] exercised an enduring influence on all subsequent discussions of human rights. Like the Declaration of Independence and the Virginia Bill of Rights of 1776, the [French] Declaration of the Rights of Man and Citizen spoke the language of "the natural, inalienable and sacred rights of man." But unlike its predecessors, it stood as the preamble to the constitution and provided the principles of political legitimacy. In the United States the Bill of Rights served to protect citizens from government and was composed only after the constitution itself was ratified; in France the declaration of rights provided the basis for government itself and was consequently drafted before the constitution.

The Declaration of the Rights of Man and Citizen laid out a vision of government based on principles completely different from those of the monarchy. According to the declaration, the legitimacy of government must now flow from the guarantee of individual rights by the law. Under the monarchy, legitimacy de-

1. The Petition of Right was a statement of civil liberties sent to King Charles I by the English Parliament. Among the rights were that the citizenry could be forced to quarter soldiers and that the people had the right of habeas corpus.

pended on the king's will and his maintenance of a historic order that granted privileges according to rank and status. Most remarkably, the deputies of 1789 endeavored to make a statement of universal application, rather than one particularly or uniquely French, and it is that universality that has ensured the continuing resonance of the document. In 1793 and again in 1795 new assemblies drew up new declarations, but these never enjoyed the prestige or authority of the 1789 declaration.

Defining Citizenship

Rather than ending debate about rights, the vote on the declaration opened it up in new ways. The very existence of an official document based on universal principles seemed to encourage further consideration. Once the principle of rights and their guarantee as the basis of government had passed into law, a crucial question shaped succeeding discussions: Who was included in the definition of a "man and citizen"? The poor, the propertyless, religious minorities, blacks, mulattoes (people of mixed race), even women? Where should the lines be drawn? The question of citizenship helped drive the Revolution into increasingly radical directions after 1789 as one excluded group after another began to assert its claims.

Throughout the nineteenth and twentieth centuries, the same issue aroused debate and provoked political conflict in every Western democracy. It remains one of the most important problems, albeit in different forms, in democracies today. Should illegal immigrants, for example, have the same rights as citizens? How long must you reside in a country to merit citizenship and full rights? How old must you be to become a full citizen? And what counts as rights: access to housing, employment, a minimum wage, abortion, or even the right to die when you choose? The variety of these modern questions shows that once rights became the basis of legitimate government, debate would inevitably shift in new directions to consider who could exercise rights and what those rights might include.

French legislators approached the question of citizenship step by step over a period of five years after 1789. Rights became the subject of so much explicit discussion in France because the political situation remained fluid—at times violently unstable—during those years. Between 1789 and 1791 the National Assembly[2] drafted legislation to establish a constitutional monarchy. To qualify for voting, men had to be property owners, but the deputies eliminated all the previous forms of legal privilege, including noble titles. An elected Legislative Assembly subsequently took office on October 1, 1791. The situation did not stabilize in 1791, however, in part because the king tried to flee to the border in disguise, in part because large numbers of former nobles left the country to form armies to combat the revolutionaries.

International and Internal Conflicts

War brought political conflicts to a head. In April 1792, France went to war with Austria (seen as an instigator of counterrevolutionary efforts) and soon lost a series of critical battles. Faced with the threat of foreign invasion, a popular uprising in Paris on August 10, 1792, forced the Legislative Assembly to depose the king from his position. The "second revolution" of August 10 opened a much more radical period in French politics. The voters elected new deputies, who promptly abolished the monarchy and established a republic. Meeting as a National Convention, the deputies tried the king for treason and ordered his execution.

The fledgling republic faced an increasingly broad and desperate war with all the major European powers, most of them monarchies deeply suspicious of republican or democratic forms of government. Between September 1792 and the election of yet another government in 1795, the National Convention ruled by a combination of laws and emergency decrees. It suppressed property qualifications for voting and eventually abolished slavery in the French colonies, but at the same time it forbade women to set up their own political clubs, established new forms of censorship, and repressed most forms of political dissent. Under a regime known as the Terror, which lasted until the end of July 1794, revolutionary tribunals sentenced thousands of opponents of the govern-

---

2. The National Assembly was the name adopted by the Estates-General (a legislative body occasionally called by the king of France) during the early stages of the revolution.

ment, male and female, to death at the newly invented guillotine. Rights and revolution therefore had a paradoxical relationship: The emergency government extended some rights in new directions (abolishing slavery) while violently suppressing others (especially freedom of speech).

After 1795, when another, still republican, constitution came into force, the political situation began to steady in some respects. The government used the guillotine much less frequently to terrorize its opponents, and it tried to rule by law rather than emergency decree. The discussion of rights, however, had reached its end; the new legislature considered turning back the clock on some issues (the deputies discussed revising or even abrogating the right to divorce made into law in 1792, for instance), but legislators found themselves too bogged down in ongoing political divisions to act decisively. Royalists wanted to reestablish the monarchy and bring back the nobility; left-wing republicans wanted to revive the political fervor of 1792–94; right-wing republicans wanted a more authoritarian form of government with strong central leadership.

In 1799, General Napoleon Bonaparte seized his opportunity in the midst of this uncertainty and took charge of an entirely new government that turned in an increasingly authoritarian, militaristic direction. In 1802 he reestablished slavery in the French colonies, and in 1804 his new Civil Code relegated women to a legally inferior status. Throughout his regime he strictly controlled the press and other publications. The glory of the nation now took precedence over the rights of the individual, although Bonaparte did guarantee freedom of religion, access to official positions based on merit, and equality before the law.

Increased Discussion of Rights

Human rights philosophy had helped to undermine the traditional monarchy, and it provided the legitimacy of the revolutionary regimes. The Declaration of the Rights of Man and Citizen announced universal principles supposedly applicable to every individual in the nation (if not in the world). The very force of its universalistic logic seemed to support, if not positively provoke, growing demands for inclusion in the political process (at least until 1794). Thus it helped push the Revolution into radical directions, but it did not by itself afford a permanent foundation for rule. There are at least two ways of looking at this predicament: Some argue that the declaration was basically sound but too far ahead of its time, that the principle of human rights gained adherents only slowly over the course of the nineteenth and twentieth centuries and is not even fully subscribed to today; others insist that the declaration and human rights philosophy itself are inherently flawed because they are too universalistic and too abstract, too out of touch with the realities of human motivation, which depend more on self-interest, religious belief, nationality, or other forms of difference distinguishing groups of people. . . .

The discussion of rights developed during the French Revolution. The debates fall into four major categories: the poor and the propertied; religious minorities; free blacks and slaves; and women. Not surprisingly, these are all in some sense social categories because most debates concerned the social qualifications necessary for citizenship. What is remarkable about this list is its extensiveness; no other eighteenth-century polity, not even the North Americans of the new United States, so explicitly discussed the rights of such a diversity of people. In the United States, for example, the question of women's rights hardly arose in public; there were no women's political clubs in the United States agitating for greater female participation and no public defenders of women's political rights among American legislators. Any discussion of women's rights in the eighteenth-century United States took place outside the halls of the legislature.

The French debates over citizenship and rights reveal a recurring clash between the ideals of human rights philosophy and the reality of eighteenth-century prejudices. Slaves, Jews, and women—to cite the most obvious examples—enjoyed political rights nowhere in the world in the eighteenth century. The mere discussion of their rights in a public forum was a novelty. What we should take from these debates, therefore, is not a sense of the backwardness of eighteenth-century views—what we would now call racism, anti-Semitism, and sexism were all very much alive and well at the time—but amazement at how many such issues French legislators felt they must publicly discuss, debate, and decide. The same prejudices shaped political life everywhere in the world at the time; what was new was the growing sentiment among French revolutionaries that changes must be made in the status of previously excluded groups. . . .

The "rights of man" was a relatively new political concept in 1789, and the leaders of the French Revolution, like those of the American Revolution before them, were not always comfortable with its implications. However discomfited, French legislators granted more far-reaching rights than any such body ever had before. Like the Americans, the French revolutionaries refused equal political rights to women, but unlike the Americans, they voted to abolish slavery and the slave trade and eventually granted equal rights, at least in principle, to all men regardless of wealth, color, or religion. Americans at that time did not abolish slavery or the slave trade, despite many voices urging abolition, and since voting qualifications remained under the jurisdiction of the states in the new United States, states could maintain property qualifications and religious tests (and most did) for citizenship. Yet despite these differences, the French and the Americans had one important thing in common: They both officially declared the equality of rights—with whatever real legal impediments—as part of their revolutions. They gave birth to an idea that would make slow but steady progress in Europe and the rest of the world during the nineteenth and twentieth centuries.

For Further Discussion

Chapter 1
1. Neither Edmund Burke nor Thomas Paine was French. How do you think their interpretations of the events of the French Revolution were affected by their English upbringings? Explain your answer.
2. After reading the viewpoints outlining the demands of the French aristocrats, middle class, and peasants, which segment of society do you believe stood to benefit the most from a revolution? Explain your answer.
3. William Doyle evaluates several of the economic remedies suggested by Charles Alexander Calonne. Which of these solutions do you think would have best solved France's financial troubles and why?

Chapter 2
1. After reading the viewpoints from Louis de Flue and Keversau, how would you describe the behavior of the French crowd during the storming of the Bastille? Explain your answer.
2. The French Republic survived for only seven years, ending when Napoleon Bonaparte, who eventually named himself emperor of France, successfully overthrew the government in 1799. In light of these facts, do you agree with Maximilien Robespierre or Joseph de Maistre's arguments on the historical importance of the founding of the French republic? Explain your answer.
3. Gwynne Lewis and François Furet disagree on the role played by the Jacobin leadership during the Reign of Terror. Whose argument do you find more convincing and why? Cite the texts when constructing your answer.

Chapter 3
1. Etta Palm d'Aelders and Louis Marie Prudhomme disagreed on whether French women should be politically active during the revolution. Which author do you believe made the more cogent argument? Why? Do you believe that Prudhomme's

viewpoint would have been more convincing if written by a woman? Explain your answers.

2. Do you agree with Anne Louis Henri de la Fare's argument that Jews living in France should not be made citizens because they are unlikely to remain loyal to any nation outside Israel? Why or why not?

3. William Doyle and Simon Schama consider which members of French society benefited most from the French Revolution. After reading their viewpoints, which groups do you believe were most positively and negatively affected and why?

Chapter 4

1. Gwynne Lewis asserts that from a capitalist standpoint, the French Revolution was only a partial success. In Jacques Solomon's opinion, the revolution offers a blueprint for socialist economies. After reading both viewpoints, which economic system do you think would have been best suited for revolutionary France? Explain your answer.

2. Darline Gay Levy, Harriet Branson Applewhite, and Mary Durham Johnson contend that the French government could not neglect the demands of France's revolutionary women. By comparison, Jane Abray asserts that these eighteenth-century feminists lacked government support. Whose conclusion do you find more convincing and why?

3. After reading the viewpoints in this chapter, what do you believe were the greatest accomplishments and greatest failings of the French Revolution?

✳ Appendix of Documents

Document 1: The Tennis Court Oath

On June 20, 1789, the National Assembly was locked out of the hall where they had previously met. The Assembly reconvened at a nearby tennis court, where they made the following oath, a vow that they would not disband until they had written a constitution.

The National Assembly, considering that it has been summoned to determine the constitution of the Kingdom, to contrive the regeneration of law and order, and to maintain true principles of monarchy; that nothing can prevent it from pursuing its deliberations in whatever place it may be forced to establish itself, and, finally, that wherever its members are gathered, there is the National Assembly;

Decrees that all members of this Assembly shall immediately swear a solemn oath not to separate, and to re-assemble wherever circumstances may necessitate, until the constitution of the Kingdom is established and consolidated on sound foundations. The said oath sworn, all members, and each of them severally, shall ratify by signature this unshakable resolution.

D.I. Wright, ed., *The French Revolution: Introductory Documents.* St. Lucia: University of Queensland Press, 1974, pp. 39–40.

Document 2: Declarations of the Rights of Man and Citizen

The Declaration of the Rights of Man and Citizen, reprinted here in its entirety, is one of the most significant human rights documents ever written. Adopted by the National Assembly on August 27, 1789, it granted numerous freedoms to French citizens, including presumption of innocence and the right to property.

The representatives of the French people, organized in National Assembly, considering that ignorance, forgetfulness or contempt of the rights of man, are the sole causes of the public miseries and of the corruption of governments, have resolved to set forth in a solemn declaration the natural, inalienable, and sacred rights of man, in order that this declaration, being ever present to all the members of the social body, may unceasingly remind them of their rights and their duties; in order that the acts of the legislative power and those of the executive power may be each moment compared with the aim of every political institution and thereby may be more respected; and in order that the demands of citizens, grounded henceforth upon simple and incontestable principles, may always take the direction of maintaining the constitution and welfare of all.

In consequence, the National Assembly recognizes and declares, in the presence and under the auspices of the Supreme Being, the following rights of man and citizen.

1. Men are born and remain free and equal in rights. Social distinctions can be based only upon public utility.

2. The aim of every political association is the preservation of the natural and imprescriptible rights of man. These rights are liberty, property, security, and resistance to oppression.

3. The source of all sovereignty is essentially in the nation; no body, no individual can exercise authority that does not proceed from it in plain terms.

4. Liberty consists in the power to do anything that does not injure others; accordingly, the exercise of the natural rights of each man has no limits except those that secure to the other members of society the enjoyment of these same rights. These limits can be determined only by law.

5. The law has the right to forbid only such actions as are injurious to society. Nothing can be forbidden that is not interdicted by the law, and no one can be constrained to do that which it does not order.

6. Law is the expression of the general will. All citizens have the right to take part personally, or by their representatives, in its formation. It must be the same for all, whether it protects or punishes. All citizens being equal in its eyes, are equally eligible to all public dignities, places, and employments, according to their capacities, and without other distinction than that of their virtues and their talents.

7. No man can be accused, arrested, or detained, except in the cases determined by the law and according to the forms that it has prescribed. Those who procure, expedite, execute, or cause to be executed arbitrary orders ought to be punished: but every citizen summoned or seized in virtue of the law ought to render instant obedience; he makes himself guilty by resistance.

8. The law ought to establish only penalties that are strictly and obviously necessary, and no one can be punished except in virtue of a law established and promulgated prior to the offence and legally applied.

9. Every man being presumed innocent until he has been pro-

nounced guilty, if it is thought indispensable to arrest him, all severity that may not be necessary to secure his person ought to be strictly suppressed by law.

10. No one should be disturbed on account of his opinions, even religious, provided their manifestation does not derange the public order established by law.

11. The free communication of ideas and opinions is one of the most precious of the rights of man; every citizen then can freely speak, write, and print, subject to responsibility for the abuse of this freedom in the cases determined by law.

12. The guarantee of the rights of man and citizen requires a public force; this force then is instituted for the advantage of all and not for the personal benefit of those to whom it is entrusted.

13. For the maintenance of the public force and for the expenses of administration a general tax is indispensable; it ought to be equally apportioned among all the citizens according to their means.

14. All the citizens have the right to ascertain, by themselves or by their representatives, the necessity of the public tax, to consent to it freely, to follow the employment of it, and to determine the quota, the assessment, the collection, and the duration of it.

15. Society has the right to call for an account of his administration from every public agent.

16. Any society in which the guarantee of the rights is not secured, or the separation of powers not determined, has no constitution at all.

17. Property being a sacred and inviolable right, no one can be deprived of it, unless a legally established public necessity evidently demands it, under the condition of a just and prior indemnity.

Diane Ravitch and Abigail Thernstrom, eds., *The Democracy Reader*. New York: HarperCollins, 1992, pp. 54–55.

Document 3: Declarations of the Rights of Woman and the Female Citizen

In 1791, Olympe de Gouges—one of the leading feminists of the French Revolution—wrote the following document, a response to Declaration of the Rights of Man and Citizen. *The following excerpt includes a list of what de Gouges believed were the political liberties and responsibilities of French women, citizens whom she believed had yet to enjoy the freedoms offered under the 1789 document.*

The Rights of Woman

Man, are you capable of being just? It is a woman who poses the question; you will not deprive her of that right at least. Tell me, what gives you sovereign empire to oppress my sex? Your strength? Your talents? Observe the Creator in his wisdom; survey in all her grandeur that nature with whom you seem to want to be in harmony, and give me, if you dare, an example of this tyrannical empire. Go back to animals, consult the elements, study plants, finally glance at all the modifications of organic matter, and surrender to the evidence when I offer you the means; search, probe, and distinguish, if you can, the sexes in the administration of nature. Everywhere you will find them mingled; everywhere they cooperate in harmonious togetherness in this immortal masterpiece.

Man alone has raised his exceptional circumstances to a principle. Bizarre, blind, bloated with science and degenerated—in a century of enlightenment and wisdom—into the crassest ignorance, he wants to command as a despot a sex which is in full possession of its intellectual faculties; he pretends to enjoy the Revolution and to claim his rights to equality in order to say nothing more about it.

Declaration of the Rights of Woman and the Female Citizen

For the National Assembly to decree in its last sessions, or in those of the next legislature:

Preamble

Mothers, daughters, sisters [and] representatives of the nation demand to be constituted into a national assembly. Believing that ignorance, omission, or scorn for the rights of woman are the only causes of public misfortunes and of the corruption of governments, [the women] have resolved to set forth in a solemn declaration the natural, inalienable, and sacred rights of woman in order that this declaration, constantly exposed before all the members of the society, will ceaselessly remind them of their rights and duties; in order that the authoritative acts of women and the authoritative acts of men may be at any moment compared with and respectful of the purpose of all political institutions; and in order that citizens' demands, henceforth based on simple and incontestable principles, will always support the constitution, good morals, and the happiness of all.

Consequently, the sex that is as superior in beauty as it is in courage during the sufferings of maternity recognizes and declares in the presence and under the auspices of the Supreme Being, the following Rights of Woman and of Female Citizens.

Article I

Woman is born free and lives equal to man in her rights. Social distinctions can be based only on the common utility.

Article II

The purpose of any political association is the conservation of the natural and imprescriptible rights of woman and man; these rights are liberty, property, security, and especially resistance to oppression.

Article III

The principle of all sovereignty rests essentially with the nation, which is nothing but the union of woman and man; no body and no individual can exercise any authority which does not come expressly from it [the nation].

Article IV

Liberty and justice consist of restoring all that belongs to others; thus, the only limits on the exercise of the natural rights of woman are perpetual male tyranny; these limits are to be reformed by the laws of nature and reason.

Article V

Laws of nature and reason proscribe all acts harmful to society; everything which is not prohibited by these wise and divine laws cannot be prevented, and no one can be constrained to do what they do not command.

Article VI

The law must be the expression of the general will; all female and male citizens must contribute either personally or through their representatives to its formation; it must be the same for all: male and female citizens, being equal in the eyes of the law, must be equally admitted to all honors, positions, and public employment according to their capacity and without other distinctions besides those of their virtues and talents.

Article VII

No woman is an exception; she is accused, arrested, and detained in cases determined by law. Women, like men, obey this rigorous law.

Article VIII

The law must establish only those penalties that are strictly and obviously necessary, and no one can be punished except by virtue of a law established and promulgated prior to the crime and legally applicable to women.

Article IX

Once any woman is declared guilty, complete rigor is [to be] exercised by the law.

Article X

No one is to be disquieted for his very basic opinions; woman has the right to mount the scaffold; she must equally have the right to mount the rostrum, provided that her demonstrations do not disturb the legally established public order.

Article XI

The free communication of thoughts and opinions is one of the most precious rights of woman, since that liberty assures the recognition of children by their fathers. Any female citizen thus may say freely, I am the mother of a child which belongs to you, without being forced by a barbarous prejudice to hide the truth; [an exception may be made] to respond to the abuse of this liberty in cases determined by the law.

Article XII

The guarantee of the rights of woman and the female citizen implies a major benefit; this guarantee must be instituted for the advantage of all, and not for the particular benefit of those to whom it is entrusted.

Article XIII

For the support of the public force and the expenses of administration, the contributions of woman and man are equal; she shares all the duties [*corvées*] and all the painful tasks; therefore, she must have the same share in the distribution of positions, employment, offices, honors, and jobs [*industrie*].

Article XIV

Female and male citizens have the right to verify, either by themselves or through their representatives, the necessity of the public contribution. This can only apply to women if they are granted an equal share, not only of wealth, but also of public administration, and in the determination of the proportion, the base, the collection, and the duration of the tax.

Article XV

The collectivity of women, joined for tax purposes to the aggregate of men, has the right to demand an accounting of his administration from any public agent.

Article XVI

No society has a constitution without the guarantee of rights and the separation of powers; the constitution is null if the majority of individuals comprising the nation have not cooperated in drafting it.

Article XVII

Property belongs to both sexes whether united or separate; for each it is an inviolable and sacred right; no one can be deprived of it, since it is the true patrimony of nature, unless the legally determined public need obviously dictates it, and then only with a just and prior indemnity.

Darline Gay Levy, Harriet Branson Applewhite, and Mary Durham Johnson, eds. and trans., *Women in Revolutionary Paris: 1789–1795*. Urbana: University of Illinois Press, 1979, pp. 89–92

Document 4: The Indictment of King Louis XVI

On December 11, 1792, France's government, the National Convention, brought thirty-three articles of indictment against the nation's former king, Louis XVI. The monarch was found guilty and beheaded on January 21, 1793. The following document details several of the articles.

Louis, the French people accuses you of having committed a multitude of crimes in order to establish your tyranny by destroying its liberty.

1. On 20 June, 1789, you attacked the sovereignty of the people by suspending the assemblies of its representatives and by driving them by violence from the place of their sessions. . . .

2. On 23 June you wished to dictate laws to the nation; you surrounded its representatives with troops; you presented them with two royal declarations, subversive of every liberty, and you ordered them to separate. Your declarations and the minutes of the Assembly establish these outrages undeniably.

3. You caused an army to march against the citizens of Paris; your satellites caused their blood to flow, and you withdrew this army only when the capture of the Bastille and the general insurrection apprised you that the people were victorious. . . .

6. For a long time you contemplated flight: on 23 February a memoir was sent to you indicating the means therefor, and you approved it. On the 28th a multitude of nobles and officers distributed themselves throughout your apartments at the Tuileries Palace to facilitate such flight. . . . On 21 June you made your escape with a false passport; you left a declaration against those same constitutional articles. . . .

7. After your arrest at Varennes, the exercise of the executive power was for a time taken from your hands; and still you conspired. . . . On 14 September you apparently accepted the Constitution; your speeches announced a desire to maintain it, and you worked to overthrow it before it even was achieved. . . .

15. Your brothers, enemies of the state, have rallied the *émigrés* under their colors; they have raised regiments, borrowed money, and contracted alliances in your name; you disavowed them only when you were quite certain that you could not harm their plans.

John H. Stewart, ed., *A Documentary Survey of the French Revolution.* New York: Macmillan, 1951, pp. 386–89.

Document 5: Napoleon Bonaparte Declares the End of the Revolution

Military mastermind Napoleon Bonaparte led a successful coup of the French government on November 10, 1799. On December 15, 1799, France's new leader issued the following proclamation, in which he stated that the French Revolution had concluded and that France now had a new and superior constitution.

Frenchmen!

A Constitution is presented to you.

It terminates the uncertainties which the provisional government introduced into external relations, into the internal and military situation of the Republic.

It places in the institutions which it establishes first magistrates whose devotion has appeared necessary for its success.

The Constitution is founded on the true principles of representative government, on the sacred rights of property, equality, and liberty.

The powers which it institutes will be strong and stable, as they must be in order to guarantee the rights of citizens and the interests of the State.

Citizens, the Revolution is established upon the principles which began it: It is ended.

Leon Bernard and Theodore B. Hodges, eds., *Readings in European History.* New York: Macmillan, 1958, pp. 349–50.

✳ Chronology

1789

> **May 5:** The Estates-General convenes at Versailles.
>
> **June 17:** The third estate declares itself the National Assembly of France.
>
> **June 20:** The members of the new Assembly swear to the so-called Tennis Court Oath.
>
> **June 27:** The king requests that all three estates meet again and votes be counted individually rather than by group.
>
> **July 14:** Paris's Bastille fortress surrenders to an angry mob.
>
> **Late July:** The so-called Great Fear spreads through the countryside, igniting widespread peasant unrest and violence.
>
> **August 4:** Responding to the peasant uprisings, the nobles in the Assembly give up most of their feudal rights.
>
> **August 27:** The Assembly adopts the Declaration of the Rights of Man and Citizen.
>
> **October 2:** Assembly leaders present the declaration to Louis for approval.
>
> **October 5–6:** When Louis delays approval of the declaration, a crowd of Parisian women march to Versailles and demand that the royal family return with them to Paris.

1791

> **June 20–24:** Louis and his family attempt to escape France but are apprehended at Varennes.
>
> **October 1:** The National Assembly having dissolved itself, the Legislative Assembly convenes its first session.

1792

> **April 20:** France declares war on Austria.
>
> **August 10:** Angry crowds break into the Tuileries Palace in Paris, forcing the royal family to flee to the safety of the Legislative Assembly.
>
> **September 20:** A French army defeats the Prussians at Valmy.
>
> **September 21:** The monarchy is abolished and the Legislative Assembly is replaced by the republican Convention.

December 15: The king is indicted on thirty-three counts of treason.

1793

January 21: The king is beheaded.

February 1: France declares war on Great Britain.

April: The Committee of Public Safety is formed and begins to assume its role as the chief organ of the Terror.

July: Robespierre joins the Committee of Public Safety.

July 13: Radical journalist Jean-Paul Marat is stabbed to death by a supporter of the Girondins.

October 16: The former queen, Marie-Antoinette, is executed.

1794

April 6: The Jacobin leader Danton is executed.

July 26: Robespierre delivers his last speech to the Convention.

July 28: Robespierre is executed; the more moderate Thermidorian Reaction begins to gain control.

1795

August 22: The five-man ruling body known as the Directory is established.

1796

March: Napoléon Bonaparte becomes general of the French army in Italy.

1797

October 18: Napoléon concludes the Treaty of Campoformio with Austria.

1798

May 19: Napoléon begins his Egyptian expedition.

1799

August 22: Napoléon departs from Egypt.

October 16: Napoléon arrives in Paris.

November 10: Napoléon and his accomplices mount a coup of the government and he becomes First Consul.

December 15: Napoléon declares that the revolution has come to an end.

For Further Research

Historical Studies

Florin Aftalion, Martin Thom, trans., *The French Revolution: An Economic Interpretation.* Cambridge, UK: Cambridge University Press, 1990.

Geoffrey Best, ed., *The Permanent Revolution: The French Revolution and Its Legacy, 1789–1989.* London: Fontana Press, 1988.

J.F. Bosher, *The French Revolution.* New York: W.W. Norton, 1988.

Marc Bouloiseau and Jonathan Mandelbaum, trans., *The Jacobin Republic, 1792–1794.* Cambridge, UK: Cambridge University Press, 1983.

Alfred Cobban, *The Social Interpretation of the French Revolution.* Cambridge, UK: Cambridge University Press, 1965.

Vincent Cronin, *Louis and Antoinette.* New York: William Morrow, 1975.

Alexis de Tocqueville and Stuart Gilbert, trans., *The Old Régime and the French Revolution.* New York: Anchor Books, 1955.

William Doyle, *Origins of the French Revolution.* Oxford, UK: Oxford University Press, 1980.

Ralph W. Greenlaw, ed., *The Economic Origins of the French Revolution: Poverty or Prosperity?* Boston: D.C. Heath, 1958.

E.J. Hobsbawm, *The Age of Revolution: 1789–1848.* New York: Mentor, 1962.

Olwen H. Hufton, *Women and the Limits of Citizenship in the French Revolution.* Toronto: University of Toronto Press, 1992.

T.A. Jackson, ed., and William Zak, trans., *Essays on the French Revolution.* London: Lawrence and Wishart, 1945.

Peter Jones, ed., *The French Revolution in Social and Political Perspective*. New York: Arnold, 1996.

Frank A. Kafker, James M. Laux, and Darline Gay Levy, eds., *The French Revolution: Conflicting Interpretations*. Malabar, FL: Krieger, 2002.

Georges Lefebvre, John Hall Stewart, and James Friguglietti, trans., *The French Revolution, Volumes I and II*. New York: Columbia University Press, 1964.

Gwynne Lewis, *The French Revolution: Rethinking the Debate*. London: Routledge, 1993.

Martin Lyons, *Napoléon Bonaparte and the Legacy of the French Revolution*. New York: St. Martin's Press, 1994.

Daniel Mornet, *French Thought in the Eighteenth Century*. North Haven, CT: Archon Books, 1969.

Steven T. Ross, ed., *The French Revolution: Conflict or Continuity?* New York: Holt, Rinehart, and Winston, 1971.

George Rudé, *The Crowd in the French Revolution*. New York: Oxford University Press, 1959.

———, *Robespierre: Portrait of a Revolutionary Democrat*. New York: Viking Press, 1976.

Simon Schama, *Citizens: A Chronicle of the French Revolution*. New York: Knopf, 1989.

Henri Sée and Edwin H. Zeydel, trans., *Economic and Social Conditions in France During the Eighteenth Century*. New York: Cooper Square, 1968.

Nora Temple, *The Road to 1789: From Reform to Revolution in France*. Cardiff: University of Wales Press, 1992.

J.M. Thompson, *Leaders of the French Revolution*. New York: Harper and Row, 1967.

Primary Sources and Document Collections

Paul H. Beik, ed. and trans., *The French Revolution*. New York: Walker, 1971.

Olivier Blanc, ed., and Alan Sheridan, trans., *Last Letters: Prisons and Prisoners of the French Revolution, 1793–1794*. New York: Farrar, Straus and Giroux, 1987.

Edmund Burke, *Reflections on the Revolution in France*. London: Penguin Books, 1986.

Peter Burley, ed., *Witness to the Revolution: American and British Commentators in France, 1788–94*. London: Weidenfeld and Nicolson, 1989.

Joseph de Maistre and Richard A. Lebrun, ed. and trans., *Considerations on France*. Cambridge, UK: Cambridge University Press, 1994.

E.L. Higgins, ed., *The French Revolution as Told by Contemporaries*. Boston: Houghton Mifflin, 1939.

Lynn Hunt, ed. and trans., *The French Revolution and Human Rights: A Brief Documentary History*. Boston: Bedford Books, 1996.

Darline Gay Levy, Harriet Branson Applewhite, and Mary Durham Johnson, eds. and trans., *Women in Revolutionary Paris, 1789–1795*. Urbana: University of Illinois Press, 1979.

Gouverneur Morris and Beatrix Cary Davenport, ed., *A Diary of the French Revolution*. Boston: Houghton Mifflin, 1939.

Thomas Paine, *The Rights of Man*. Dutton: New York, 1979.

Pierre Louis Roederer and Murray Forsyth, ed. and trans., *The Spirit of the Revolution of 1789*. Brookfield, VT: Scolar Press, 1989.

Helen Maria Williams, *Letters Written in France*. Oxford, UK: Woodstock Books, 1989.

Websites

Internet Modern History Sourcebook: French Revolution, www.fordham.edu/halsall/mod/modsbook13.html. This site is part of the Internet History Sourcebooks Project, which consists of collections of historical and public domain texts on a variety of historical topics. The French Revolution site, which provides information on the revolution and Napoléon Bonaparte, was compiled and edited by history professor Paul Halsall.

Liberty, Equality, Fraternity: Exploring the French Revolution, http://chnm.gmu.edu/revolution/index.html. This website is a collaboration between the Center for History and New Media and the American Social History Project. It offers more than three hundred primary documents, songs, maps, images, and topical essays.

✳ Index

218